PROBLEMS AS
possibilities

Problem-Based

Learning for

K–16 Education

2nd Edition

LINDA TORP AND SARA SAGE

Association for Supervision and Curriculum Development
Alexandria, Virginia USA

Association for Supervision and Curriculum Development
1703 N. Beauregard St. • Alexandria, VA 22311-1714 USA
Telephone: 1-800-933-2723 or 703-578-9600 • Fax: 703-575-5400
Web site: http://www.ascd.org • E-mail: member@ascd.org

ASCD publications present a variety of viewpoints. The views expressed or implied in this book should not be interpreted as official positions of the Association.

Printed in the United States of America.

ASCD Product No. 101064   s1/2002
ASCD member price: $18.95   nonmember price: $22.95

Library of Congress Cataloging-in-Publication Data
Torp, Linda, 1946–
     Problems as possibilities : problem-based learning for K–16 education /
Linda Torp, Sara Sage.— 2nd ed.
     p. cm.
Includes bibliographical references and index.
ISBN 0-87120-574-2 (alk. paper)
1. Problem-based learning.   2. Curriculum planning.   I. Sage, Sara, 1961–   .   II. Title.
     LB1027.42 .T67 2002
     375′.001—dc21

                                                                                    2001006219

06 05 04 03   10 9 8 7 6 5 4 3 2

Problems as Possibilities:
Problem-Based Learning for K–16 Education

2nd Edition

List of Figures

In Memory of
Bernard C. Hollister

Bernard C. Hollister, master teacher, thinker, and friend, contributed greatly to our lives—both personally and professionally. He was a man of vision, commitment, and humor, always striving to empower learners of all ages through his probing and penetrating style of engagement. Like Don Quixote, he dreamed big and conquered much in the service of teaching and learning—and was truly an original. Though we miss Bernie's presence in our lives, his spirit lives on through the many learners he mentored. We are fortunate to be able to count ourselves among them.

—Linda Torp and Sara Sage

ACKNOWLEDGMENTS

We are grateful to the Illinois Mathematics and Science Academy (IMSA) and its Center for Problem-Based Learning, which served as a catalyst for the ideas in this book. We would also like to thank the Harris Family Foundation for their generous support of our work.

Numerous individuals affiliated with the Center@IMSA have contributed to the conceptual and developmental process of understanding problem-based learning, and we have all learned from each other. We particularly thank the staff of the Center, IMSA faculty (past and present), and those teachers with whom we have partnered in Illinois and other states. Our editors at ASCD provided us with helpful feedback, which enabled us to express our understandings effectively, and helped facilitate the entire process. Thanks to all of you!

Introduction to the 2nd Edition

We can't put it together. It is together.
—S. Brand, *The Last Whole Earth Catalog* (1971)

WHETHER THINKING ABOUT THE UNIVERSE, THE AMBIGUI-
ties of life, or the wonders of learning, educators realize that the whole is so
much more than any collection of parts. As they work with learners of all
ages, educators constantly strive to create holistic and connected experiences that enable students to tackle the complexities facing them as citizens
in a global community, as well as in everyday situations. These experiences
should reveal a need to be open-minded and adaptable and should consider
the interrelatedness of systems, both natural and contrived.

We journey through life encountering, grappling with, and resolving
problems that present powerful opportunities for learning. Ask people to

describe a time in their lives when they really learned something that they remember today with understanding. Most people will not recall a formal educational experience. They will, however, relate struggling with a problem such as dealing with the death of a parent. *What needs to be done? Who needs to know? How will we cope with the news? Is there an estate or mounting liabilities? What are the legal issues?* These types of questions beg consideration and a balanced response.

Messy, ill-structured problems capture our attention and draw us into their depths. They focus our investigation and thinking, bringing us closer and closer to comprehension and resolution. These problems present holistic learning experiences. They expose and connect rich content and essential skills. They catalyze critical and creative thinking, and they place us in situations that demand decisions based upon sound criteria, taking into account conflicting interests and incomplete information. We're talking, of course, about problem-based learning—where the problem comes first and learning is fueled through the problem's investigation and resolution.

Since 1992 the Center for Problem-Based Learning at the Illinois Mathematics and Science Academy (IMSA) has investigated and applied the principles of problem-based learning (PBL). Our work there has described how problem-based learning is applied in elementary, middle, and high school settings. We have measured the effects of defined aspects of a problem-based approach, and we have shared our experience and learning with educators across the country. In 1998 the Center for Problem-Based Learn-

ing became an integral part of the Center for the Advancement and Renewal of Learning and Teaching: The Center @ IMSA. (See the Appendix for more information.)

This book is a natural extension of the work at IMSA. But how do we represent a dynamic concept like problem-based learning in a way that enables understanding and encourages application? What can we relate on the static pages of a book that would meet the needs of a diverse group of learners?

In thinking through our problem as authors, we heard clearly the voices of educators with whom we have worked. Their needs were as diverse as their interests. Some were captivated by stories of real classroom experiences. "What happened? Why were the students intrigued by the problem?" Others wanted to know about problem-based learning. "Where did PBL come from? How does it relate to other ideas about teaching and learning that are part of the educational scene?" Many desired to become involved from the inside and design their own problem-based units. "Where do I begin to create my own PBL curriculum? How do I coach the learning process?" Today's reality of local, state, and national standards complicates these issues. "How can I fairly and adequately assess learning targeted by and acquired through problem-based learning experiences?" We've found that each of these approaches to teaching about problem-based learning has value for the reader.

Our book offers opportunities to learn about PBL from multiple perspectives. The diverse members of our audience will find strong connections to their own classroom experience while reading about problem-based learning.

For people who want to experience PBL, Chapter 1 provides anecdotal reports of teachers and students. Vignettes from several grade levels and contexts enable readers to see PBL's possibilities. This second edition includes examples from universities, as well as elementary and secondary education (thus, as the title of this book indicates, PBL can apply to kindergarten through "grade" 16, or college level).

For readers who want to learn more about the theory behind this approach to education, Chapter 2 provides an overview of problem-based learning, and Chapter 3 presents background information. We hope these chapters supply answers for those who need to know what PBL is and where it comes from.

When you're ready to try designing and implementing PBL, Chapters 4, 5, and 6 show you how to play with an idea and make it your own. These chapters present practical information to enable educators to create and develop PBL curriculum and plan for instruction in a PBL classroom.

Chapter 7 adds to our understanding of assessment in and through PBL. This chapter presents the grounding for the assessment of PBL experiences guided and supported by a standards-based approach—one that recognizes individual accountability for learning and demonstrating proficiency much the same way as a musician performs or an athlete competes. Some day we all have to suit up and step onto the playing field. After our students graduate or drop out, it's too late for the guided practice they deserve.

For educators who need to know the "whys" to find their way through an idea, Chapter 8 offers answers, building a solid foundation for PBL as a valuable innovation for today's learners and opening the door to the process of becoming a teacher of PBL.

Different pathways through these chapters help serve the needs of different learners:

- If you are intrigued by context and how ideas play themselves out in authentic settings, begin with Chapter 1.
- If you want to know the origins and the grounding of ideas, begin with Chapter 2, 3, or 8.
- And if you must roll up your sleeves and become immersed immediately in the "how" of things, begin with Chapter 4, 5, 6, or 7.

Wherever you begin (see Figure I.1), make sure you read the whole book to experience all the aspects of problem-based learning as a natural integrating focus for relevant curriculum and meaningful student learning.

FIGURE I.1
Overview of *Problems as Possibilities*

Designing and Implementing PBL
◆ Chapter 4: What is our model for PBL?

◆ Chapter 5: How do you design a PBL curriculum?
  • Teacher as designer
  • Teacher as refiner

◆ Chapter 6: How do you implement PBL?
  • Teacher as coach
  • Students as active problem-solvers

Assessing in PBL
◆ Chapter 7: How do you assess learning in and through PBL?
  • Teacher as assessor
  • Students as performers
    ⇒ Demonstrating skill proficiency
    ⇒ Demonstrating thinking and reasoning
    ⇒ Demonstrating knowledge application

Thinking about PBL
◆ Chapter 8: How do you support PBL?
  • What are your questions?
  • What does it take to become a teacher of PBL?

Learning About PBL
◆ Chapter 2: What is PBL?
  • Background
  • Comparison of PBL to other instructional strategies
◆ Chapter 3: What are the foundations of PBL?

Experiencing PBL
◆ Chapter 1: What does PBL look like in real classrooms?
  • Through the eyes of learners
  • Through the eyes of teachers

Adapted from Torp & Sage (1998), p. 4.

1

WHAT DOES PROBLEM-BASED LEARNING LOOK LIKE IN CLASSROOMS?

To educate is to take seriously both the quest for life's meaning and the meaning of individual lives. . . . Through telling, writing, reading, and listening to life stories—one's own and others'—those engaged in this work [teaching] can penetrate cultural barriers, discover the power of the self and the integrity of the other, and deepen their understanding of their respective histories and possibilities.

—Witherell & Noddings (1991)

AS WE WORK WITH EDUCATORS AROUND THE COUNTRY, WE have come to appreciate the power of story. Strong connections develop when we relate how teachers organize problem-based learning (PBL) experiences and how students respond to them. Our partners are enthusiastic and thoughtful PBL practitioners from whom we learn a great deal. We'll begin with their words—their stories.

At Elementary Schools

One important story is unfolding at Westgate Elementary School in Arlington Heights, Illinois. Educators there have used PBL for a number of years, examining how it works best with young students and adapting the process to a point where their school community—administrators, teachers, students, parents, and businesspeople—enthusiastically support the method.

In one problem, 1st through 5th grade students investigated difficulties their former principal was having maintaining a healthy flower garden at home. Students examined soil and plant samples from her garden, read about how to grow healthy plants, searched the Internet, contacted local experts, and conducted experiments on growing plants under different conditions.

Several students had difficulty with adults who wouldn't take them seriously when they tried to find information to help them investigate their problem. Michael, a 4th grader, called a local plant nursery for information about watering plants. The person answering the phone said, "Just don't give them too much water," and then hung up.

Students discussed his dilemma. Andy suggested that Michael should have called back and asked, "How much water is too much?" or kept the person on the phone by saying, "Wait a second," or something similar. Eventually the group located an individual who would answer questions to their satisfaction. Students learned something about perseverance and differences among adults.

Teachers at Westgate are excited about how students are learning, and students are excited about their learning. Here are their comments:

> The way they're doing their experiments and thinking about their experiments before they just rush into doing them—they're reading them over and predicting and deciding whether they're going to be helpful or not—they've definitely surpassed my expectations at this point.
> —Linda Zakarian, 1st/2nd grade teacher

> I saw the kids learn a ton of information about plants, and they know that if they're going to have a garden, they need to really read directions, and they need to know some conditions of sunlight and water. They got out of it what I wanted them to get out of it. They're much more knowledgeable about plants, but I didn't have to do it from a textbook. . . . I've learned to constantly push the kids to keep thinking. If they come up with one answer, don't stop there, because the likelihood is there are at least five more answers.
> —Melissa Rabin, 3rd/4th grade teacher

> [Things have to work together] like the sun and the water. You have to know if it's going to rain or not, and you have to know where to plant your flowers so they get the right amount of sun or shade they need. I think it's weird that sometimes things don't need very much sun but they need a lot of water.
> —Richard, 4th grade student*

*All student names are fictitious.

Both students and teachers enjoy the authenticity of PBL, as shown in these comments:

> I like PBL because it's challenging and fun, because you're learning something new. Every problem's a little different 'cause you're going for different goals in the solutions.
>
> —Cal, 4th grade student

> Some kids question when you're teaching basic skills: "Why do we have to learn this? When are we ever going to do this?" [With PBL] you're showing them a reason—a specific, real-life situation. I'm teaching them basic skills, but I'm giving them a reason.
>
> —Linda Zakarian, 1st/2nd grade teacher

Ruth, a student in Zakarian's class, said she liked the plant problem because she could help the former principal solve a real problem. Ruth's mother echoed her daughter's excitement:

> Ruth talked a lot about the plant problem; we discussed it a lot. I was impressed with the sources they went to for information, phone calls they made; [they even went] as far as getting an analysis of the soil—that they would *think* about that. Also, I could see on her face that she was very thrilled that she was able to find out information that an adult was very interested in . . . but also that she just received this level of respect from an adult. It really boosted her confidence. . . . I think problem-based learning empowers children to be real active participants in the world around them when they get the opportunity.

As we interviewed students, we found they identified other skills they had worked on during PBL experiences. They described how they helped each other locate and understand information in the plant problem:

> [I use a highlighter pen] if there's a picture there with a whole bunch of things. . . . You can highlight [some parts] so you won't need to keep reading it; it tells you what you're reading.
>
> —Jennifer, 1st grade student

> Some of the people [in my group] looked at pictures and got a little information; then if I read and found something, I would think: *Would that make sense? Is it important or not?* Sometimes it would be important for *this* but not important for *this* . . . like all the stuff I read in this book about seeds—I found that animals help scatter seeds; that is important. But the picture was showing a bird taking a cherry, so I wasn't sure [if that was important] because [the principal] might not have any of those kinds of trees.
>
> —Kristen, 2nd grade student

Students completed a pre-test and a post-test in which they were asked to develop instructions on how to grow plants successfully. For her pre-test, Andrea, a 3rd grader, drew four pictures, with little accompanying information (mentioning seeds, sun, and rain). On a post-test in May, however, seven months after completing the plant problem, Andrea wrote instructions that included 10 necessary components for healthy plant growth: "soil, seeds, water, fertilizer, sun, rain, carbon dioxide, respiration/breathe, chlorophyll/food, and space to grow" (all spelled correctly). Andrea, by the way, is a special education student.

Many members of the learning community at Westgate report that they can spot by their behavior students who have had several experiences with PBL. These students are better at dealing with conflicts in the lunchroom or on the playground. They also approach learning differently in the classroom, asking more questions and refusing to let go of issues until they are satisfied they understand the issues thoroughly, even to the extent of assigning themselves homework. Christine Ortlund, another experienced PBL teacher at Westgate, mentions that many students now don't just *ask* to learn by solving problems, they actually *demand* it.

At Middle Schools

An essential part of the middle school story is to find engaging, authentic problems where students are placed in roles and situations that hook them—at this age, they are typically interested in everything *but* academics. Middle school researchers stress the importance of relating middle school curriculum to issues of student concern and interest (for example, Beane [1993]). One former team of middle school teachers—Karoline Krynock and Louise Robb—realized the power of incorporating student interest through problem-based learning:

> If you give them [8th grade students] a role of
> power, then they really buy into this. We've done two
> problems where kids have been put in the position of

making recommendations . . . about school district policy to school board members, a superintendent, and a principal. And [the students] walked away from that saying, "We could say something. We had something to say and adults listened to us. . . . We may have actually done something for our school—something that's really going to directly affect us."

> —Karoline Krynock, Mason, OH;
> former science teacher, Barrington Middle School,
> Prairie Campus, Barrington, IL

Sage, Krynock, and Robb (2000) detail one problem the latter two researchers designed involving prairie restoration on their school campus. About this problem, students said:

> It's not just something for school—it went farther
> than that. It was, like, for the town.
> —Sherry, 8th grade student

> I like this more than a regular English class—more
> than just going in and getting reading stories and doing
> grammar.
> —Mike, 8th grade student

> It [PBL] got more interesting. We just started
> working with a solution, and it was less boring than
> sitting in a classroom listening to a speaker.
> —Roger, 8th grade student

Another problem required students to design a mass transit system from Chicago to Northwest Indiana "over, under, or through 57 miles of Lake Michigan" (Krynock & Robb, 1999). These open-ended problems not only pique student interest but also teach the curriculum. The two teachers

(Krynock & Robb, 1996) conducted classroom research showing that their PBL students learned as much or more content in a problem designed around the issue of possible genetic causes for aggressive behavior than did students in a more traditional genetics unit. Krynock says that her students learn more "real science" in PBL than in any other teaching method she has used.

Dealing with authentic problems helps students think about ethical aspects of issues they might not have otherwise considered. At the end of a PBL experience dealing with HIV/AIDS, Krynock reported that her class felt a strong obligation to educate others to reduce fear surrounding the disease. She was surprised and impressed by their maturity and empathy in considering how an HIV-positive student might feel and their subsequent desire to be proactive in providing education to their peers:

> Even if we had read a hundred short stories and memorized a million AIDS pamphlets, I don't know that they would have learned the valuable lessons they learned from the short [time] we spent examining this problem.
> —Karoline Krynock, Mason, OH;
> former science teacher, Barrington Middle School,
> Prairie Campus, Barrington, IL

Lisa Nicholson, a special education teacher at Burr Ridge Middle School in Burr Ridge, Illinois, has found that PBL is an effective strategy to use with a wide range of students. Nicholson coteaches several problems—one is on deer overpopulation in their area, and another is HIV-positive middle school students. She says that although all students benefit from the real-life problems the teachers have presented in PBL, special education students are particularly well suited to the approach, because they often don't want to learn or they have difficulty learning unless they see a reason behind the lesson. PBL also allows students to use the learning style that is best for them. Furthermore, they can demonstrate their knowledge through many different assessment formats, such as oral presentations, debates, and posters.

At High Schools

Consider this problem designed as a precursor to reading *To Kill a Mockingbird*:

> Students are members of the Alabama Historical Society, which has been contracted to research a family's background during the time period of the novel *To Kill a Mockingbird*. What was going on in the family during the time period of the novel? How reliable is the information the historical society uncovers? If controversial information about family members arises, who needs to know—or not?
> —Yolanda Willis, language arts teacher,
> East Aurora High School, Aurora, IL

Even though her students normally enjoyed this book, Willis reports that PBL enhanced this American literature unit:

> I think the kids were more *into* what they were doing; it seemed more relevant to them, especially with the social studies teacher [an expert on the 1930s]

coming in and talking with them. . . . What really grabbed them . . . was when I brought the guy in who said that the original person the students were researching had lynched *his* grandfather. So then it became more of an ethical problem—the kids had to go back to their problem statement and decide: "Maybe we shouldn't even be doing this." Before that, it was: "Okay, we'll do this; we'll do all the research and make all the pictures." But when [that ethical dimension] came in, they were like, "Wow!" It really blew them away.

Teachers can design PBL problems around interdisciplinary issues as well. Another teacher relates this story of student empowerment:

> There's a metamorphosis that you cannot even begin to contemplate. I listened to one girl who was being interviewed by the [*Chicago Tribune*] on the phone. Crissy said, "I never knew I could do all this; I didn't know I was such a good thinker; I didn't used to be able to get up in front of people and speak. . . ." I love to see the depth of their thinking and hear realizations that they're operating on a different level. . . . I like to see the metamorphosis in staff that is the audience for their exhibitions. Administrators are seeing kids differently. Other teachers are saying, "Yes, kids can do." I've always believed kids can do anything, but it's so exciting to see that happen.
>
> —Ellen Jo Ljung, language arts teacher, Glenbard West High School, Glen Ellyn, IL

Real-life problems can become PBL problems, as shown in these examples:

- Bernard Hollister, a former social science teacher, co-taught a PBL course, Science, Society, and the Future (SSF), for seniors at the Illinois Mathematics and Science Academy (IMSA). One year, SSF students started with a problem Hollister designed around lunchroom waste in U.S. schools. As he put it, students began "stripping away the layers of the onion" when they discovered that lunchroom waste was only the tip of this problem. The real problem seemed to be flawed methodology and strong political motivations in the congressional study they were using.

- Also at IMSA, science/physics teacher David Workman has used PBL for a number of years. One problem unit in his integrated science course revolved around finding the best possible design for retention/detention ponds in the immediate school vicinity. Severe flooding had occurred in the community in the previous year. In this course, students investigate "problem platforms," which expose physical and biological problematic contexts—such as pond life or habitation on Mars. Such exposure allows student involvement in several different PBL experiences.

- John Thompson, an IMSA science/biology teacher, uses PBL in several science classes. For a predator unit in his ecology class, Thompson focuses on the central issue of wolf reintroduction into natural habitats. Each year he updates this core problem to reflect a current real-world scenario.

- A science/chemistry instructor, Richard Dods, has developed a biochemistry course around realistic problem scenarios, such as learning about isoenzymes by diagnosing, as cardiologists, the source of chest pain in the character Miles Silverberg from television's "Murphy Brown."

High school students participating in PBL clearly enjoy the strategy and find PBL beneficial in preparing them for their future:

> I like Comm-Tech [a communications technology course] because it's a class where you take all the material you've learned and you use it. . . . Other classes teach you *what* to learn; this class teaches you *how* to learn. I think I'll actually use this class when I move on into computer science and electrical engineering; it teaches you how to solve problems on the job.
> —Don, student in Ellen Ljung's class, Glenbard West High School, Glen Ellyn, IL

> [PBL] is a different approach to education. Instead of: "Here's a sheet of vocabulary words, memorize them," you could say, "Well, this happens, you know—why? Now go find out. See what you can find out about the why or the how of something. . . ." There's usually not one right answer. There can be more than one answer, or there isn't one; you form a new question and go from there.
> —Cindy, student in John Thompson's ecology class, Illinois Mathematics and Science Academy, Aurora, IL

> The skills I learned in [John Thompson's] ecology class have been helpful both in terms of the research and studying that I've done for my college courses and also the research that I've done for my own research career. . . . That series of thought processes that takes

you from complete ignorance to a knowledge that's focused and can answer a specific question is a very useful thing to know, and it's a very difficult skill to learn, I think, in most school settings.
> —Elizabeth Pine, former IMSA student, 1993 Westinghouse Science Talent Search Competition award winner

At Universities

PBL is a fast-growing strategy in both undergraduate and graduate education. In working with undergraduates, we are finding a variety of courses and disciplines that apply PBL. As two examples, the University of Delaware and Samford University in Birmingham, Alabama, have committed to using PBL across disciplines and levels.

Several professors at Samford University are using PBL in teacher education. Becky Atkinson and Martha Ralls of Samford teach a middle school course with Joy Brown, a local middle school principal. They begin their course for prospective middle school teachers with the problem "Our Unique Students," in which the preservice teachers create profiles for a typical class of 25 middle school students (Atkinson, Brown, & Ralls, 2000). Using fictitious but realistic student profiles, the education students then move on to such problems as "Team Goals and Mission" (creating and communicating yearlong goals to students and parents), "Different Strokes" (considering the special needs of a diverse student population), and "Active Learning" (selecting, implementing, and evaluating active teaching strategies in an actual middle school classroom with experienced classroom teachers as mentors). PBL benefited not only the students but also the instructors. Here are instructor comments:

> I was amazed at watching PBL in action; watching them process the problems—whether we were trying to facilitate their processing or not, it was just remarkable. It's so powerful. I was a little envious that my own teachers haven't been through this training. . . . In the end they [Samford students] learned what middle school was like. The goals of the course are to have them appreciate and differentiate middle school from elementary and high school; the course goals were accomplished. They learned it heart and mind.
> —Joy Brown, principal,
> Robert F. Bumpus Middle School, Birmingham, AL

> I didn't feel like I had to know all the answers, but I felt as though I needed to at least have stumbled across the same questions the students had. So I found myself thinking, OK, *what if I'm a 20-year-old, and I've never had a child?* I was remembering how I was when I was first teaching. . . . So I learned that I don't always have to have the right answer as long as I have fully explored what the questions could be.
> —Becky Atkinson, adjunct instructor of education,
> Samford University

> [The best thing I saw about this PBL experience was] interest. They were engaged; their eyes lit up. They were on a search for the answer; they wanted to know. This was real life—it was interesting; it challenged them. I had been through this class many times before; this level of interest was unusual.
> —Martha Ralls, professor of education,
> Samford University

Carol Dean, assistant professor of education at Samford University, teaches a foundations course to preservice teachers in which she uses current education problems in the news as the basis for PBL in her class. The problems focus on issues like teaching as a profession, tenure for K–12 teachers, vouchers, and school funding. In one recent problem ("No Lottery! Now What?"), Dean (2000) asked students to consider the school funding situation in Alabama, where a state lottery proposal had just failed. Students, in small groups, responded to a real call for letters in the local paper by crafting a plan to improve equitable funding to schools.

Also at Samford University, George Keller teaches a section of a problem-based course, Scientific Methods, required for all nonscience majors. His students work on "hot topic" problems like the science behind low-carbohydrate diets, genetically altered foods, the necessity of various vaccines, strategies for reducing the rate of HIV/AIDS in intravenous drug users, and so forth. Keller sees PBL as a way to offer students a new approach to science:

> I think the biggest thing is that [PBL] is a new way to present science that isn't fact, fact, explanation, fact, fact, fact—they see that science is a process. . . . It's a different way of thinking about science, of appreciating both the power and the limitations of it.
> —George Keller, associate professor of biology,
> Samford University, Birmingham, AL

At the University of Delaware, Deborah Allen, Linda Dion, and Hal White (2000) work with a peer facilitator program to assist in large undergraduate PBL classes in the basic and applied sciences, humanities, and the social sciences. Peer facilitators—students who have already taken and done well in the various courses—work with one or several small groups to facilitate discussion, problem solving, and group communication. In White's Introduction to Biochemistry course, peer facilitators report a statistically significant increase in their library research, writing, communication, and problem-solving skills from the tutoring experience (Allen, Dion, & White, 2000).

Several colleges and universities are applying problem-based approaches in undergraduate mathematics courses. At Indiana University South Bend, Morteza Shafii-Mousavi, associate professor of mathematics, and Paul Kochanowski, professor of economics, have cotaught the freshman level course Math in Action: Social and Industrial Problems for several years (Shafii-Mousavi & Kochanowski, 1999). Students, in small groups, work with various community organizations and businesses each spring to help solve a real problem. Recent issues included examining the efficiency of food preparation and distribution in an area school district, analyzing the survey results of a gifted program in another district, maximizing the usage of a property surrounding a mall, and determining the optimal mix of fund-raising activities for a local nonprofit organization.

Students in this course report some of the following benefits (Kochanowski, Sage, & Shafii-Mousavi, 2000):

- Seeing how math problems apply directly to life problems.
- Learning computer skills with math.
- Learning about graphs and how data fit into them.
- Using their creative sides and other skills besides math.
- Putting a project together from material learned in class.
- Applying math tools to real-life problems.
- Being able to demonstrate knowledge instead of taking a test.
- Directly applying knowledge for someone, which made the procedures "stick."

In a similar mathematics course taught at the University of South Carolina Spartanburg, a longitudinal study comparing 68 sections (problem-based and traditional sections) showed the median success rate (considered the number passing as a percent of initial enrollment) was 75 percent for problem-based sections and 56 percent for traditional sections (Ulmer, 1999).

* * *

Stories from teachers, students, parents, principals, and researchers are powerful. But what is this thing called problem-based learning? What do we know about PBL? What do teachers and students do in PBL? How can you design problems for your class? How can you write your own PBL story? You'll find these questions and others addressed as you investigate PBL in this book.

2

WHAT IS
PROBLEM-BASED LEARNING?

NEARLY EVERY DAY, WE FACE POSSIBILITIES AND PROBLEMS that affect our personal and professional lives. The ability not only to cope but also to identify key issues, access information, and effectively work our way through these situations contributes to success in whatever we pursue. Building a mental network of these experiences enables us to make connections through association and interpretation. This "context-building knowledge gives form to everything we do or think or feel, on the job, in the voting booth, in the home" (Broudy, 1982, p. 578).

Most teachers are familiar with models in which students learn identified content and processes through lecture, direct instruction, and guided discovery. Then they apply this new learning in well-structured situations, problem sets, and forced-response items designed to see if they understand or have mastered the lesson. This instructional paradigm, with a teach, learn, and apply sequence, has been the standard in our schools for quite some time. Roles are clear: Teachers teach; students learn. If only the process were that simple.

Problem-based learning refocuses our practice to what some call a learning paradigm. PBL confronts students with a messy, ill-structured situation in which they assume the role of the stakeholder or "owner" of this situation. They identify the real problem and learn whatever is necessary to arrive at a viable solution through investigation. Teachers use real-world problems as they coach learning through probing, questioning, and challenging student thinking. Here are some examples:

> Second grade students serve as advisors to NASA. A planet much like Earth has experienced massive destruction of the elements in its biosphere. What is causing the destruction of plant life? Can new plants from Earth be successfully introduced to help save the planet's environment? How can we find out?
> —Rawls Byrd Elementary School, Williamsburg, VA

> Middle school students act as scientists with the State Department of Nuclear Safety. Some people in a small community feel their health is at risk because a company keeps thorium piled above ground at one of their plants. What are the critical issues? Who else is concerned? What is the extent of our authority? What action, if any, should be taken?
> —Summer Challenge Program, Illinois Mathematics and Science Academy, Aurora, IL

> High school basic composition students serve as consultants to the warden of a women's correctional facility. They examine the potential causes of recidivism among women prisoners. Why don't these women succeed in society? What communication skills would help the women improve their chances? How can these "consultants" design a program to address prisoners' needs?
> —East Aurora High School, Aurora, IL

Defining Problem-Based Learning

Problem-based learning is focused, experiential learning (minds-on, hands-on) organized around the investigation and resolution of messy, real-world problems. PBL—which incorporates two complementary processes, *curriculum organization* and *instructional strategy*—includes three main characteristics:

- Engages students as stakeholders in a problem situation.
- Organizes curriculum around a given holistic problem, enabling student learning in relevant and connected ways.
- Creates a learning environment in which teachers coach student thinking and guide student inquiry, facilitating deeper levels of understanding.

PBL provides authentic experiences that foster active learning, support knowledge construction, and naturally integrate school learning and real life; this curriculum approach also addresses state and national standards and integrates disciplines. The problematic situation offers the center around which curriculum is organized, attracting and sustaining students' interest with its need for resolution while exposing multiple perspectives. Students are engaged problem solvers, identifying the root problem and the conditions needed for a good solution, pursuing meaning and understanding, and becoming self-directed learners. Teachers are problem-solving colleagues who model interest and enthusiasm for learning and are also cognitive coaches who nurture an environment that supports open inquiry (see Figure 2.1).

Overview of PBL Design and Implementation

Designing and implementing a PBL unit are interrelated processes that balance the needs of students, the curriculum, and learning standards within a particular learning context. Figure 2.2 shows the main elements in the two processes.

Problem Design

Teachers select possibilities for problem situations by knowing their curriculum, being aware of learning standards, scanning local newspapers, and speaking with community members and colleagues (see Figure 2.3). They think about the characteristics and needs of their learners, looking for ways to hook students:

> The problematic situation has the seeds of interest within it. Students can relate to people attempting to

deal with the unknown and living under adverse conditions. (Barell, 1995a, p. 122)

In considering possible problems for study, teachers assess opportunities for "curriculum payback," including integrating across disciplines and making community connections.

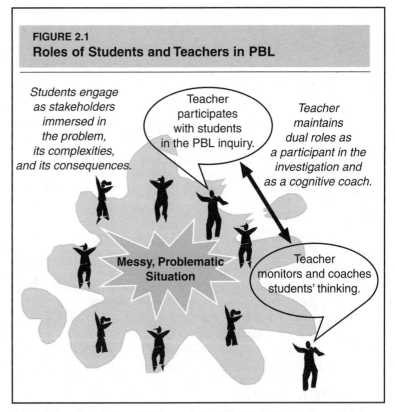

FIGURE 2.1
Roles of Students and Teachers in PBL

Students engage as stakeholders immersed in the problem, its complexities, and its consequences.

Teacher participates with students in the PBL inquiry.

Teacher maintains dual roles as a participant in the investigation and as a cognitive coach.

Messy, Problematic Situation

Teacher monitors and coaches students' thinking.

Adapted from Torp & Sage (1998), p. 16. © 1995 Illinois Mathematics and Science Academy, Center for Problem-Based Learning, Aurora, IL.

This exploration leads to identifying a problem that will enable students to make meaningful connections between school and life while providing educators with powerful curricular connections:

> Problematic situations are robust in that they contain within them significant concepts worth thinking about. (Barell, 1995a, p. 131)

Educators seek out or design scenarios that provide rich opportunities for demonstrating learning through projects, presentations, or other means authentic to the situation. The added benefit is that students' work closely mirrors more integrated, complex, and authentic activity—activity that is inherently motivating. State and national standards also target these types of engaged learning activities. Consider an excerpt from the Illinois Learning Standards' Applications of Learning for Language Arts, shown in Figure 2.4.

Problem-based learning surrounds students with opportunities to develop proficiency in applications of learning that set them apart from other students. Even more beneficial is that this profi-

ciency supports achievement in all academic areas. Figure 2.5 shows a graphic representation of the PBL process.

To develop a PBL unit, teachers decide upon the learning focus and a role to frame the students' involvement in a chosen problem. "The learning experience provides students with opportunities to take different perspectives on the subject" (Barell, 1995a, p. 123). Which perspective will intrigue students and provide the greatest opportunity for

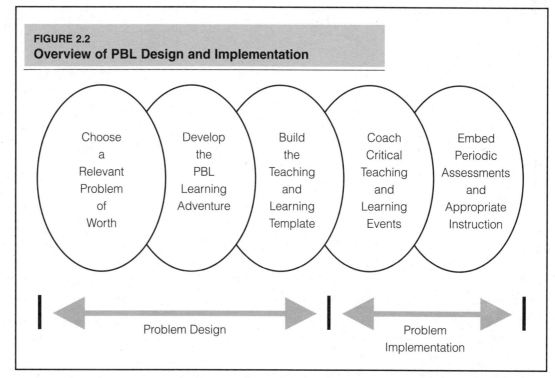

FIGURE 2.2
Overview of PBL Design and Implementation

Choose a Relevant Problem of Worth

Develop the PBL Learning Adventure

Build the Teaching and Learning Template

Coach Critical Teaching and Learning Events

Embed Periodic Assessments and Appropriate Instruction

Problem Design

Problem Implementation

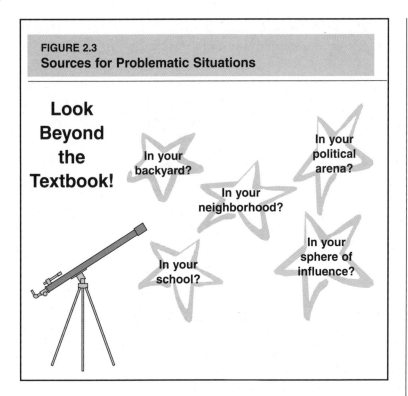

FIGURE 2.3
Sources for Problematic Situations

Look Beyond the Textbook!

In your backyard?

In your political arena?

In your neighborhood?

In your school?

In your sphere of influence?

FIGURE 2.4
Excerpt from Illinois Learning Standards' Applications of Learning for Language Arts

APPLICATIONS OF LEARNING. Students demonstrate and deepen their understanding of basic knowledge and skills. These applied learning skills cross academic disciplines and reinforce the important learning of the disciplines.

✓ **Solving Problems.** *Recognize and investigate problems; formulate and propose solutions supported by reason and evidence.*
This demands that students read and listen, comprehend ideas, ask and answer questions, convey their ideas through written and oral means, and explain their reasoning.

✓ **Communicating.** *Express and interpret information and ideas.*
Individuals and groups exchange ideas and information— oral and written—at lunch tables; through newspapers and magazines; and through radio, television, and online computer services.

✓ **Using Technology.** *Use appropriate instruments, electronic equipment, computers and networks to access information, process ideas, and communicate results.*

✓ **Working on Teams.** *Learn and contribute productively as individuals and as members of groups.*
Students must speak clearly and listen well as they share ideas, plans, instructions, and evaluations. In researching and bringing outside information to a team, they must search, select, and understand a variety of sources.

✓ **Making Connections.** *Recognize and apply connections of important information and ideas within and among learning areas.*

Source: Illinois State Board of Education. (1997). *Illinois learning standards.* Springfield, IL: Author. Available: http://www.isbe.state.il.us/ils/standards.html

engagement? We want students to own the problem and the inquiry, and to have a personal investment in the solution.

A shift in perspective can profoundly affect problem resolution. Imagine how different the problem of the endangered spotted owl in old-growth forests in the Pacific Northwest appears from the perspective of legislator, lumberman, environmentalist, and retailer in a local community.

Unit development also includes selecting appropriate information and community resources, and creating materials to support student learning.

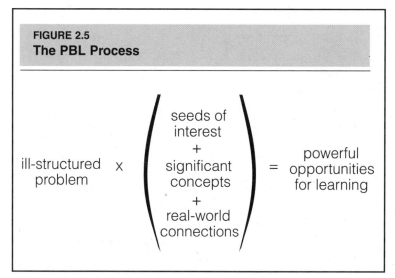

FIGURE 2.5
The PBL Process

ill-structured problem × (seeds of interest + significant concepts + real-world connections) = powerful opportunities for learning

Source: Adapted from Torp & Sage (1998, p. 15).

Problem Implementation

Planning for instruction requires an appreciation of the teaching and learning events of PBL, along with an understanding of the teacher's role as cognitive coach. Through hundreds of classroom observations, we have found several events that are essential for successful PBL experiences. As teachers construct a teaching and learning template, they have for each event clear goals that support student thinking at different levels. As teachers coach students toward these goals, they anticipate embedding essential instruction and assessment at critical points during problem investigation. We detail these teaching and learning events in Chapter 4, but for now, let's consider the natural flow of problem-based learning as students meet, investigate, and resolve a problem.

The Flow of a PBL Learning Experience

Students assume the role of a stakeholder in the problem scenario. We want our learners to step inside the learning situation and own the problem. In their role they naturally should have some say in the outcome or resolution. If they are to make recommendations to the mayor about traffic flow during a major event in their city, which role would provide them a greater voice or influence—as members of the transportation department? Downtown retailers? Middle school students?

Students need not shift roles for every problem. What if their school needs major renovation and a building addition? Who better to examine the school's physical environment in relation to the learning needs of middle grade students, and to make recommendations to the architect and school board? What is important is that the role and situation are complementary and provide a platform for influencing the outcome.

Students should also make an empathic connection with the situation; in other words, we want them to care about what happens. Sylwester (1995) states:

> We know emotion is very important to the educative process because it drives attention, which drives learning and memory. (p. 72)

Later he goes on to say:

> By separating emotion from logic and reason in the classroom, we've simplified school management and evaluation, but we've also then separated two sides of one coin—and lost something important in the process. (p. 75)

Students are immersed in an ill-structured problematic situation. Such a situation is messy and complex. Not enough information is provided, so the situation requires inquiry, information gathering, and reflection. As information is gathered and evaluated, the root problem or puzzlement may change, opening up new avenues for investigation. Students uncover diverging assumptions, conflicting evidence, and varying opinions about the situation. Even when students decide upon a solution, multiple options for achieving it are probably available. A problematic situation is changing, tentative, and has no simple or fixed solution.

Why, then, do we center PBL on these types of problems? Matthew Lipman (1991) in *Thinking in Education* makes a strong argument in favor of ill-structured problems:

> Where students have no sense that anything has been left out or is incomplete, they have no need to go beyond the information given. In contrast, the partial, the fragmentary, and the problematic taunt us to complete them or resolve them. (p. 68)

Students must analyze, synthesize, and evaluate to gain a sense of the whole and formulate a viable solution. Well-structured problems, on the other hand, provide the information, the compass, and a clear destination for the problem solver, tapping only the lower-level thinking skills of knowledge, comprehension, and application.

What does such work mean for younger students? Do we hold back PBL experiences until children near middle school age? Not at all. Primary grade students engage in PBL scenarios with a vigor and enthusiasm that surprises and delights their teachers. These children are not limited by the notion that all information is located between the covers of an encyclopedia. They pursue information by phoning, questioning, and experimenting. Like good investigators, they know the value of probing beyond first-level answers by asking "Why?" again and again and again. Problematic scenarios appropriate for younger students abound. Just as beauty lies in the eye of the beholder, what makes something a problem resides in the mind of the learner.

For example, a problem scenario described in Chapter 1 explains how 1st graders helped their former principal solve the mystery of why her garden wouldn't grow properly. They learned more about plants, growth, and conditions for life than they would have from any story and windowsill garden. What's more important, they experienced the critical connection between learning and life.

Students identify what they know, what they need to know, and their ideas. From what they understand about their role, the situation, and the limited information provided, students clarify and share what they know at the outset of the PBL assignment. This process helps them access prior knowledge and begin to make connections. The ill-structured problem compels students to identify what they know and need to know to resolve the tension of a problem situation (Boud & Feletti, 1991). Almost concurrently, they begin to comprehend the situation more fully. From this point, a natural progression occurs to categorize information needs and potential sources while parceling out tasks.

Teachers may be concerned about students taking a wrong turn or going down a blind alley as they plan or gather information. Students will, on occasion, do just that. But in doing so, they will undoubtedly learn from the experience. Often, knowing what doesn't work or apply in a given situation is every bit as valuable as knowing what does. The messiness of authentic problem solving—including an occasionally seemingly nonproductive detour—yields rich learning:

> Students in a summer youth program worked at an area forest preserve. In years past, they were given explicit directions about the building and placement of bat houses within the preserve. Following a shift to a PBL program frame, students were challenged to accomplish the same goal, but this time, they investigated the native bats and their habitat, designed the bat houses, and placed them appropriately. Despite this need for inquiry coupled with predictable meandering, these students accomplished a great deal more with noticeable interest and enthusiasm when the goal was problematized as compared to when the goals were explicit. (Benoit, 1996)

Students define the problem to focus further investigation. Once students are immersed in their role and the problematic situation, they gather and share information among the other class members or their team. This activity enables everyone involved to gain a holistic understanding of the problem. The information-collecting process often takes on a life of its own: Students pursue intriguing threads, personal interests take over, and the inquiry becomes blurred. Coaching students to come to a clear statement of what they believe to be the central issue of the problem, along with a list of several conditions that must be satisfied for a good solution, is essential. Many teachers with whom we work post evolving problem statements in the classroom to help tighten and target the investigation.

Students will likely engage in more than one cycle of inquiry—sharing what they have discovered, identifying what else they need to know, and refining their problem statement as they learn more—before they are ready to consider some sort of resolution. Motivated by their inquiry, students become self-directed learners. A key is to interest them in the learning experience:

> Teaching is generally a delightful experience when we focus on activities that student brains enjoy doing and do well, such as exploring concepts, creating metaphors, estimating and predicting, cooperating on group tasks, and discussing moral or ethical issues. (Sylwester, 1995, p. 119)

Students generate several possible solutions and identify the one that fits best. With appropriate coaching, students discuss an emerging picture of the real problem, perhaps several times, before they are ready to generate possible solutions. After developing the solutions, students evaluate them in light of the problem statement's central issue and identified conditions. According to Sylwester (1995), the brain is well suited for this type of activity:

> Our brain is currently much better than a computer at conceptualizing ambiguous problems—at identifying definitive and value-laden elements that it can incorporate into an acceptable general solution. (p. 119)

Once students select the solution that fits best, they prepare to present their findings. They may choose to share the problem and their solution by using concept maps, charts, graphs, proposals, position papers, memos, maps, models, videos, or a home page on the World Wide Web—whatever is authentic to their role and the situation. Students offer this solution in a performance assessment situation, ideally interacting with the problem's real stakeholders and responding to stakeholder questions and concerns. If appropriate, these stakeholders may even implement the solution.

For example, students at Steinmetz High School in Chicago participated in a problem-based service learning project. They identified a problem at a local hospital within their community. The hospital had recently located some biohazardous waste that had been stored since the 1930s. The students took on the problem and investigated its legal, ethical, waste management, and health concerns. They arrived at a viable solution and presented it to the hospital board. The board adopted their proposal.

As an engagement process, problem-based learning empowers students as learners and doers to translate imagination and thought into actuality as well as to reflect on the process and proposed solution. As a process, problem-based learning provides multiple and varied opportunities to apply essential knowledge and skills that are stressed in local, state, and national standards.

What Are the Essential Elements of Problem-Based Learning?

Although many formats for presenting and implementing PBL units are possible, the following parameters remain consistent:

The problematic situation is presented first and serves as the organizing center and context for learning.

The problematic situation has common characteristics:
- It is ill-structured and messy.
- It often changes with the addition of new information.
- It is not solved easily or with a specific formula.
- It does not result in one right answer.

Students are active problem solvers and learners; teachers are cognitive and metacognitive coaches.

Information is shared, but knowledge is a personal construction of the learner. Discussion and challenge expose and test thinking.

Assessment is an authentic companion to the problem and process.

A PBL unit is not necessarily interdisciplinary, but it is always integrative.

What Are the Benefits of Problem-Based Learning?

Although PBL plays out differently as settings vary from primary to graduate classrooms, particular benefits surface at all levels. At the Illinois Mathematics and Science Academy (IMSA), a core group of teachers has designed and implemented problem-based learning units and courses since the early 1990s. Their experiences and reflections coupled with findings from the research literature present a profile of PBL's benefits (see Gallagher, Rosenthal, & Stepien, 1992; Stepien & Gallagher, 1993; Barell, 1998). We highlight the benefits here and provide teacher comments that describe their experiences with PBL.

PBL Increases Motivation

PBL engages students in learning through the attraction or pull of problem dissonance or tension. They take on more and delve deeper as they make a personal investment in the outcome of their inquiry. Teacher comments attest to this involvement:

> The most important thing that happened to me is that when I got involved in doing problem-based learning, it was so obvious to me—the difference in the way in which students approached their own responsibilities and activities in the classroom compared to the way students did when I used other methods. . . . They just did different things. I think it was important to me to *see* that they did different things, because it was clear to me that for their learning to change they *had* to do different things.
> —David Workman, science/physics teacher, Illinois Mathematics and Science Academy, Aurora, IL

> It's so much more exciting to see real learning going on. And it's real—you know, where the kids are really hungry to learn. A kid came back up to me the next day and said, "I went over to the city library and checked out *Uncle Tom's Cabin* on my own." He didn't act like it was a big thing; I thought it was pretty amazing! That book is 140 years old or something, and he was wading through it.
> —Kris Hightshoe, social studies teacher, Edison Middle School, Champaign, IL

PBL Makes Learning Relevant to the Real World

PBL offers students an obvious answer to the questions, "Why do we need to learn this information?" and "What does what I am doing in school have to do with anything in the real world?" Teacher comments show how learning relevant material in schools affects students:

The last two days, I've had my students out doing orienteering. They really enjoyed it. Now in hindsight, I see that problem-based learning is a lot like orienteering through a problem. What I discovered was that I would get them going and they would scurry into the woods with their compasses and try to find the various answers or points that they were seeking. . . . When they came back, there was this great rejoicing in their own accomplishment. I can't imagine how I could have explained it or the kind of lecture I would have had to give to explain those points in the woods that would have received the same kind of reaction as their actually doing it. . . . There was a problem; the problem was that they find [the point]; when they found it, it was like they had beaten the system. The woods had not beaten them. To me, that's not a bad comparison to what problem-based [learning] is. You go into the wilderness and once you find those things, there is a joy of discovery. I don't know that the joy of being told is nearly as great.

—John Thompson, science/biology teacher,
Illinois Mathematics and Science Academy, Aurora, IL

Suddenly the students have real tasks to do and real reasons to want to learn about things. People are taking them seriously as learners; it's not just a mock situation.

—Lori Hinton, 4th/5th grade teacher,
Westgate Elementary School, Arlington Heights, IL

PBL Promotes Higher-Order Thinking

Coupled with cognitive coaching strategies, the ill-structured problem scenario calls upon critical and creative thinking by suspending the guessing game of, "What's the right answer the teacher wants me to find?" Students gather information significant to the problem, assessing its credibil-

ity and validity. In bringing the problem to acceptable closure with evidence to support decisions, students are held to high benchmarks of thinking. Teachers work to encourage such thinking:

We've had some panels of experts come in and hear solutions from our groups. The adults are just astounded by the depth and breadth of [the students'] knowledge and the kinds of things they've been able to deal with. Even experts came in as resources, thinking they were going to give a canned speech and left [only] five minutes for questions. I said, "Excuse me, but could you present for five minutes, and then we'll have an hour of questions?" . . . The kids are asking incredibly complex questions that show they have a lot of understanding of content.

—Louise Robb, language arts teacher,
Barrington Middle School, Prairie Campus,
Barrington, IL

You've got to get used to being able to reflect back the question—bounce it right back—rather than feel the necessity to give the answer. That's not easy to do.

—Richard Dods, science/chemistry teacher,
Illinois Mathematics and Science Academy, Aurora, IL

PBL Encourages Learning How to Learn

PBL promotes metacognition and self-regulated learning. Students generate strategies for problem definition, information gathering, data analysis, and hypothesis building and testing. Then they share and compare those strategies with the strategies of other students and mentors. Such challenging work goes on at all grade levels:

I think it's critical for a kid to be able to formulate the process: "That's what I know and that's what I need to know." If they can begin to think about how they are thinking that way, they could know either where to get the stuff or add to whatever they know. . . . They are much more adaptable—now I'm going to start talking like an ecologist here—but their ability to adapt to whatever intellectual or challenging environment they are put in is lots better. Was it Pasteur who said, "Chance favors the prepared mind"? The question is, how do you prepare the mind? Is it simply by knowing more stuff? Or knowing how to approach the problem?

—John Thompson, science/biology teacher,
Illinois Mathematics and Science Academy, Aurora, IL

First graders are not inhibited. They're ready to hit the phones, go on the Internet, and go ask their neighbors. They are open to inquiry, and they're not afraid of that challenge. They're able to define for themselves aspects of the work that interest and challenge them. . . . It's a whole new way for these kids to not just be able to think, but to do.

—Emily Alford, former principal,
Westgate Elementary School, Arlington Heights, IL

PBL Requires Authenticity

PBL engages student learning in ways that are similar to real-world situations and assesses learning in ways that demonstrate understanding and not mere replication. Teachers report on the results of providing authentic situations and assessment:

It wasn't clear to me how powerful the method was until almost two-thirds of the way through that first year, when it became obvious that significant groups of

kids were taking off totally on their own and going in powerful directions that we had hoped would occur, but weren't guaranteed would occur. And the kids kept coming to us and saying that this is the way it ought to be. They were doing things that were just astonishing. I still remember—[a student]—who went off to the conference on the West Coast. She became . . . in a year one of the prime experts on ELF (electromagnetic low frequency) fields and biological systems in the country. She knew as much as the experts.

—David Workman, science/physics teacher,
Illinois Mathematics and Science Academy, Aurora, IL

Simulated problems certainly can have value, but how can you compare a simulation with the power of real-world problem solving that has genuine results? Some of my students were able to convince a previously adamantly opposed village board to allow a pilot run for a local dance club, while others developed a Web site and brochure for a local pet shelter to help it gain needed publicity.

—Ellen Jo Ljung, language arts teacher,
Glenbard West High School, Glen Ellyn, IL

A Landscape of Instructional Strategies

In thinking about the benefits of PBL and viewing students as knowers, thinkers, and doers, we have chosen to differentiate problem-based learning from a range of instructional strategies. We know that each strategy has its place in a teacher's instructional repertoire, and we see clear differences when considering the role of the student, teacher, and problem, along with other key factors (see Figure 2.6).

FIGURE 2.6
Comparison of Instructional Strategies

TYPE OF INSTRUCTION	ROLE OF THE TEACHER	ROLE OF THE STUDENT	COGNITIVE FOCUS	METACOGNITIVE FOCUS	ROLE IN THE PROBLEM	PROBLEM	INFORMATION
Lecture	As expert: • Directs thinking • Holds knowledge • Evaluates students	As receiver: • Inert • Inactive • Empty	Students replicate received knowledge and apply in testing situation.	None: Study skills are the responsibility of the student.	As a student: Learns about things outside personal experience or "over there" (Heathcote & Herbert, 1980).	• Well structured • Presented as a challenge to retention	Organized and presented by instructor.
Direct Instruction	As conductor: • Orchestrates learning • Guides rehearsal • Evaluates students	As follower: • Responsive • Semi-active • Waits for teacher's lead	Students practice and replicate received knowledge and apply in testing situation.	Guided practice provides tacit focus upon strategies.	As a student: Learns about things outside personal experience or "over there" (Heathcote & Herbert, 1980).	• Well structured • Presented as a challenge to retention	Organized and presented by instructor.
Case Method	As consultant: • Lectures • Sets the environment • Advises • Evaluates students	As client: • Responsive • Semi-active • Applies own experience	Students apply received knowledge and own experience in case resolution.	Strategies learned are applied to cases, not necessarily independently.	As a student: Learns about things outside personal experience or "over there" (Heathcote & Herbert, 1980).	• Well structured • Presented as a challenge to application and analysis	Most is organized and presented by instructor.
Discovery-Based Inquiry	As mystery writer: • Combines parts that lead to discovery • Provides clues and foreshadows events • Evaluates students	As detective: • Picks up clues • Semi-active • Seeks out evidence	Students apply "discovered" truths to the construction of other constructs and principles.	Inquiry process learned is applied to investigations, not necessarily independently.	As a student: Learns about things outside personal experience or "over there" (Heathcote & Herbert, 1980).	• Well structured • Presented as a strategy for knowledge construction	Most is organized and presented by instructor.
Problem-Centered Learning	As resource: • Explicitly teaches content and problem solving • Poses problems to which students relate • Translates into students' world • Evaluates students	As problem solver: • Evaluates resources • Crafts divergent solutions • Active	Students synthesize received knowledge and individuality in the resolution of problems within curricular context.	Problem-solving process learned is applied to problems, not necessarily independently.	As a student: Learns about things outside personal experience or "over there" (Heathcote & Herbert, 1980).	• Moderately structured • Presented as a strategy to develop effective learning behaviors	Most is organized and presented by instructor.

FIGURE 2.6—*CONTINUED*
Comparison of Instructional Strategies

Type of Instruction	Role of the Teacher	Role of the Student	Cognitive Focus	Metacognitive Focus	Role in the Problem	Problem	Information
Simulation and Gaming	As stage manager: • Manages situation • Sets simulation/game in motion • Watches from the wings • Debriefs situation	As player: • Experiences simulation/game • Reacts to emergent conditions/variables • Active	Students learn about themselves, their roles in life situations, and about the reality modeled.	• Learning exposed during the debriefing process. • Experience interpreted and evaluated in reflection.	As a player or pawn: Reacts to events that are part of personal experience or "here" to relate to things "over there" (Heathcote & Herbert, 1980).	• Moderately structured • Presented as a strategy to understand self and events	Most is organized and presented by instructor.
Mantle of the Expert (Roles)	As travel agent: • Enables learning from within group • Maps ways in which students will discover what they need to know to complete task • Guides their journey • Debriefs situation	As traveler: • Actively experiences the journey • Acts within and through a historical perspective	Students reconstruct classroom communication, creating a dialectic where they learn at the conceptual, personal, and social levels.	• The eminent pressure of the lived experience activates prior learning. • Teacher simultaneously models and coaches.	As a doer: Walks in the time of the event, learning about events "here" (Heathcote & Herbert, 1980).	• Tightly focused, but somewhat ill-structured • Presented as a situation that demands interaction with the social system	Most is organized and presented by instructor.
Problem-Based Learning	As coach: • Presents problematic situation • Models, coaches, and fades • Engages in the process as coinvestigator • Assesses learning	As participant: • Actively grapples with the complexity of the situation • Investigates and resolves problem from the inside	Students synthesize and construct knowledge to bring resolution to problems in a way that meets the conditions that they themselves set forth.	• Teacher models and coaches as needed. • Students develop strategies to enable and direct their own learning.	As a stakeholder: Immerses in the situation, learning about events "here" (Heathcote & Herbert, 1980).	• Ill-structured • Presented as a situation within which a compelling problem is yet to be defined	Little is presented by instructor without students identifying a need to know. Most is gathered and analyzed by students.

References: Alkove & McCarthy, 1992; Casey & Tucker, 1994; Cornbleth, 1988; Doll, 1993; Heathcote, 1983; Heathcote & Herbert, 1980; Lederman, 1994; Swink, 1993; Wagner, 1988; Willems, 1981; Wolf, McIlvain, & Stockburger, 1992.

Summary

We have described what problem-based learning is and how it develops student dispositions toward inquiry and decision making based on evidence, not assertion. Both from the literature and our experience, we know that, in PBL, students gather and apply knowledge and skills from multiple disciplines and sources as they assess an array of plausible solutions for a relevant ill-structured problem. The products and presentations of their investigations provide evidence of learning and skill acquisition—and assessment of individual performance against standards. In the next chapter, we delve into the background of PBL and examine how PBL enables students to emerge as open-minded, adaptable, complex thinkers able to assess creatively and critically the ever-changing world around them.

3

WHAT ARE THE FOUNDATIONS OF PROBLEM-BASED LEARNING?

STUDENTS LEARN FROM REAL ACTIVITY (GLICKMAN, 1991). The simplicity and logic of this statement have been embraced, researched, and written about for nearly a century. PBL is a form of experiential education in which learners think, know, and do in an authentic context. Widely used in medical and business education for several decades, PBL has been present in K–16 education for several years. But the core of PBL—students as active problem solvers, making their own meaning—is an educational tradition dating back to John Dewey. To understand the foundations of PBL, we turn first to medical education, and then in more depth to PBL's constructivist roots in K–16 education.

Beginnings at the Medical School Level

Problem-based learning as a distinct educational concept has its origins in medical education in the 1960s. At that time, clinical medical educators at

McMaster University in Ontario, Canada, became increasingly concerned with a student's ability to recall and apply in clinical settings biomedical content knowledge and skills taught (and presumably learned) in previous biomedical coursework. Learning through lecture did not equate well with application; furthermore, grades, although valued indicators of success, were not good predictors of a student's ability to apply that knowledge in clinical situations with real patients (Albanese & Mitchell, 1993). This situation—reproduce for the test and soon forget—is familiar to all of us.

As a consequence, educators at McMaster designed a program that placed students in small tutorial groups where they interacted with simulated patients whose reports of medical problems were blurred by patient anxiety, incomplete information, and the frailties of interpersonal communication. They used patient interviews, records, and selected laboratory results to identify learning issues and develop a diagnosis and treatment plan. A discussion-based approach that faculty tutors facilitated brought students into the inquiry and learning process as full participants rather than as mere receptors (Barrows & Tamblyn, 1976).

In the 1970s, the University of New Mexico, with the support of colleagues from McMaster University, began a small PBL program side-by-side with the pre-existing traditional program. Mounting comparative evidence showed clearly that the PBL students were learning as much content as the traditional students, thus easing some initial discomfort with coverage issues. Studies also found students in the new program less threatened by their environment and more able to pursue learning independently, an indication that they were equipped to be lifelong learners (Aspy, Aspy, & Quinby, 1993).

In the 1980s, Harvard University Medical School's New Pathways Program adopted a problem-based learning format for one of its four learning societies of 40 students. The 1990s saw other medical schools moving toward problem-based learning—Southern Illinois University, Rush, Bowman Gray, Tufts, Michigan State, and University of Hawaii, to name a few (Aspy, Aspy, & Quinby, 1993).

Information-processing theory supports to a large degree problem-based learning in medical schools. The central ideas of information-processing theory are that the learning situation

- Activates prior knowledge, facilitating new learning.
- Parallels ways in which this knowledge will be needed in real-world situations.
- Increases the probability that the learner will recall and apply what is stored in memory.

For people studying to become physicians, their roles and the problematic situations into which they are immersed as learners are clear. Learning situations and application situations are directly related. Students who assume the role of doctors attending to the needs of their patients *will become* doctors attending to the needs of their patients. As they learn, they accumulate a bank of cues that serve to trigger memory and activate knowledge associated with learning situations. Information processing is an efficient and effective accessing and flow of information (Perkins, 1992). Such work, though, does not eliminate the possibility for a great deal of ambiguity and uncertainty in comforting, counseling, and caring for patients.

Foundations in K–16 Education

In K–16 settings, the needs of learners and the psychological foundation we propose for PBL are significantly different than for medical students. K–16 students also need to recall and apply what they have learned, but we cannot predict as assuredly as for medical students the setting in which learning will be applied. Our students may go on to become teachers, engineers, secretaries, programmers, perhaps even doctors. We may never know, but we are charged, nevertheless, with preparing them to face their futures. We also know little about what K–16 students truly know when they walk into our classrooms. We must facilitate a wide range of cognitive activity inherent in answering these questions:

- What do our learners bring to the situation?
- What do they do with it?
- What do they walk away with?

In other words, students must do and think. As David Perkins (1992) points out, "If students do not learn to think with the knowledge they are stockpiling, they might as well not have it" (p. 30). To be able to think in that way, students need to understand at deeper levels, and to understand at deeper levels they need to engage in sustained thinking about topics or issues—to crawl inside ideas and expose misconceptions while making multiple connections. From this intimate perspective, students become knowers

and doers and thinkers, adapting and integrating new learning in the process.

J. G. Brooks and Brooks (1999) cite Greenberg's (1990) four criteria for a good problem-solving situation as exemplars of a constructivist approach:

- Students make a testable prediction.
- Students can use available or easily accessible materials.
- The situation itself is complex enough to support varied approaches and generate multiple solutions.
- The problem-solving process is enhanced, not hindered, by a collaborative approach.

Brooks and Brooks extend these criteria with the additional criterion of relevance: Students see a link, whether inherent in the situation or mediated by the teacher, between their situation and the real world. "Posing problems of emerging relevance is a guiding principle of constructivist pedagogy" (Brooks, J. G., & Brooks, 1999, p. 35).

Why Constructivism?

Various professional organizations and groups within education are defining curriculum standards and desired learning outcomes within a more constructivist framework. Such a framework suggests posing relevant problems to learners and structuring learning around primary concepts (for example, in science, see the *National Science Education Standards* [National Research Council, 1996] and the *Benchmarks for Science Literacy* [American Association for the

Advancement of Science, Project 2061, 1993]). Other groups define a need for competence in not only basic skills and personal qualities but also thinking skills—such as solving problems, reasoning, and knowing how to learn (for example, see U.S. Department of Labor, 1991).

Such a major change in education involves replacing the whole educational system (Reigeluth, 1994). Earlier in this century, when employers valued compliance and workers who knew how to perform discrete tasks, our bureaucratic, centralized, hierarchical educational system fit the bill. Today, however, in an information age, social scientists generally agree that people will work in teams in more democratic organizations and will need to be able to take personal initiative and integrate tasks. According to Reigeluth, emerging features for a new educational system for this information age include cooperative learning, thinking, problem-solving skills and meaning making, and communication skills. The teacher in the information-age environment will serve more as a coach or facilitator of learning, rather than as a lecturer or drill-and-response instructor. These features sound a great deal like the features of problem-based learning.

A Brief Look at Constructivist Theory and Practice

During the Progressive Era, Dewey (1916) saw the tackling of significant problems as the ultimate way to engage learners in meaning making and problem solving. He further believed that learning should be situated within the context of community (Dewey, 1943). Interest in such open inquiry, activity-based, and integrative approaches in our classrooms has grown in recent years. These types of approaches are sometimes called constructivism (Brooks, J. G., & Brooks, 1999).

Constructivist Theory

Constructivism is a philosophical view on how people come to understand or know. The idea that knowledge is constructed in the minds of learners is not new; today the work of philosopher Richard Rorty (1991) perhaps best characterizes this concept. Rorty presents knowledge, not as a representation of the real world or a "match" between knowledge and reality, but rather as a collection of conceptual structures that are adapted, or viable, within a person's range of experience. In other words, the person's knowledge "fits" with the world, much like how a key fits a lock (Bodner, 1986). Each of us builds our own key by making sense of the world, and many different keys can open a given lock.

Constructivist theory in education comes primarily from the work of John Dewey and Jean Piaget. Working from this idea that learners construct their own knowledge, both Dewey and Piaget contended that the stimulus for learning is some experience of cognitive conflict, or "puzzlement" (Savery & Duffy, 1995). Dewey argued that learning should prepare a person for life, not simply for work. He proposed that learning should be organized around the interests of the learner and that learning is an active effort by learners interested in resolving particular issues. Piaget proposed that cognitive change and learning take place when a learner's way of thinking, or scheme, leads to perturbation instead of producing what the learner expects. This perturbation (puzzlement) then leads to accommodation (cognitive change) and a new sense of equilibrium.

Cognitive change often results from interactions with other learners who may hold different understandings (von Glasersfeld, 1989). These social interactions may challenge our current views as well as allow us to test our current understandings to see how well they help us make sense of and function in our world (Savery & Duffy, 1995). Learners bring their own suppositions to learning experiences based on what fits their experiences. For example, a learner might believe that "nothing is left but the taste" when sugar dissolves in hot water. This supposition will likely hold with that learner unless she can construct a new supposition that more appropriately explains her experience with sugar and water and can be supported with evidence (Bodner, 1986).

A Constructivist Educational Model

Every day, millions of students enter school wanting to learn, hoping to be stimulated, engaged, and treated well, and hoping to find meaning in what they do. And every day that we, as educators, stimulate and challenge our students to focus their minds on meaningful tasks, to think about important issues, and to construct new understandings of their worlds, we—and they—achieve a meaningful victory.

—Brooks, J. G., & Brooks (1999, p. 120)

A constructivist model of learning might include a number of approaches. Consider the following recommendations, based on the work of numerous authors:

- Posing learning around larger tasks or problems relevant to students.
- Structuring learning around primary concepts.
- Supporting the learner working in a complex, authentic environment.
- Seeking and valuing students' points of view.
- Assessing student learning in the context of teaching and incorporating self-assessment.
- Supporting and challenging student thinking through cognitive coaching.
- Encouraging collaborative groups for testing student ideas against alternative views.
- Encouraging the use of alternative and primary sources for information.
- Adapting curriculum to address student questions and ideas.

In a constructivist social science classroom, for example, a high school teacher uses several of the preceding recommendations to plan a PBL experience on how social policies in the 1980s affected the economic and educational profile of the African American population in the United States (Brooks, J. G., & Brooks, 1993). Instead of reading a textbook, students are coached to interpret census reports obtained from the Internet and to generate their own hypotheses about social policies. Teachers often use census or other demographic data on a variety of topics, such as characteristics of U.S. presidents, or data on cases of the plague in the 20th century as the stimulus for learning and meaning making in their classes.

Constructivism and Problem-Based Learning

Problem-based learning may be one of the best exemplars of a constructivist learning environment (Savery & Duffy, 1995). The design of engaging, ill-structured problem scenarios for K–16 students, which is described in Chapter 4, exemplifies several important constructivist principles. J. G. Brooks and Brooks (1999) stress the importance of centering learning around such problems:

> We realized that the nature of questions posed to students greatly influences the depth to which the students search for answers. Posing problems of emerging relevance and searching for windows into students' thinking form a particular frame of reference about the role of the teacher and about the teaching process. It cannot be included in a teacher's repertoire as an add-on. It must be a basic element of that repertoire. (p. 44)

Implementing PBL in K–16 classrooms requires teachers to assume the role of coach and students to be active learners and problem solvers. As teachers model and coach strong cognitive and metacognitive behaviors and dispositions, students learn how to learn and become excited about learning through problem solving. Von Glasersfeld (1993) indicates that we can show students how thinking one's way to a solution can provide a personal satisfaction, thus generating the motivation to learn more.

Summary

PBL—a powerful strategy for curriculum, instruction, and assessment—has rich foundations both in experiential learning theory and philosophy and at the professional school level. Having laid this foundation, we proceed in the next chapters to explore PBL in more detail. We examine teaching and learning events in PBL, the design of PBL experiences, and the implementation of PBL in real classrooms.

4

WHAT IS OUR MODEL FOR PROBLEM-BASED LEARNING?

DURING THE PAST EIGHT YEARS, WE HAVE DESIGNED AND developed PBL units and courses, shared our experiences with educators and PBL experts around the world, and engaged in research to describe and assess the effects of PBL in K–16 education. Now one of the authors has moved into private enterprise and the other into university life, but we are still working with teachers and students and still very much committed to PBL. Such work has informed our thinking and contributed to a picture of PBL as practiced in K–16 settings. This model of the important processes of PBL—design and implementation—fits well with a constructivist model of teaching and learning. Just how exactly does it fit? This chapter outlines our model of the teaching and learning events in PBL.

Teaching and Learning Events in PBL

The teaching and learning events in problem-based learning are designed to promote active student learning and provide a scaffolding of the teaching and learning process for educators. The events generate important learning issues around a carefully crafted problem situation so that students can work through the issues in authentic and rigorous ways. These events are not necessarily rigid, fixed, or strictly sequenced. Learners may revisit parts of the PBL process, particularly *defining the problem statement* and *gathering and sharing information* (described in this chapter), as they delve deeper into the problem. A colleague likens the process to "stripping away the layers of the onion":

> As learners explore the problem, their knowledge base increases as they find new and different sources of information about the problem. Of course, a learner could stop at any layer of the problem and offer solutions. It is the job of the teacher/coach to push learners to keep stripping away the layers of the onion so that the learners are not comfortable with just simplistic problem statements.
>
> —Bernard Hollister, social science teacher, former instructor at Illinois Mathematics and Science Academy, Aurora, IL

In Hollister's comments, we also hear evidence of the critical role that the teacher/coach plays in problem-based learning. As we stated in Chapter 2, problem-based learning is a model composed of two complementary processes that go hand in hand: curriculum organization and instructional strategy. Figure 4.1 shows the instructional strategy component, including the teaching and learning events essential for PBL experiences.

FIGURE 4.1
Instructional Template for a PBL Unit

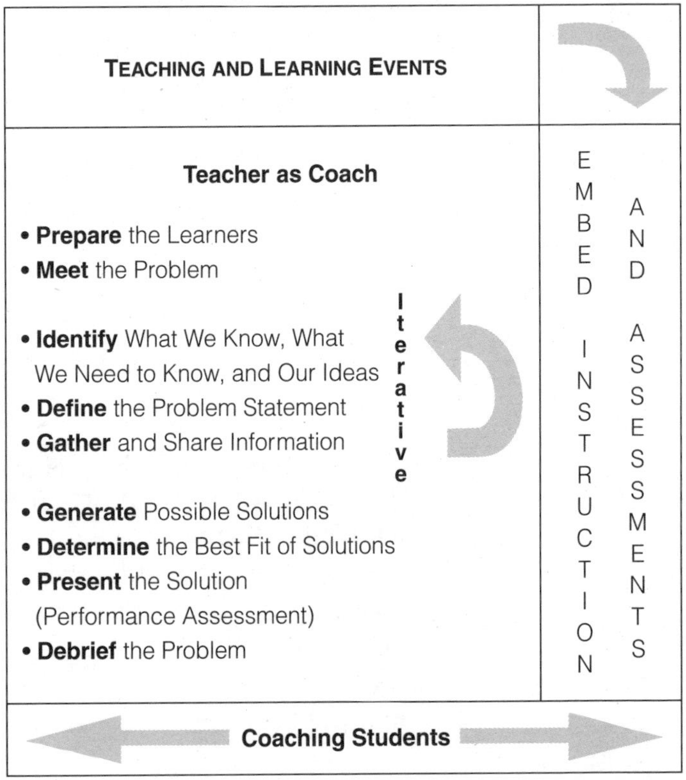

TEACHING AND LEARNING EVENTS

Teacher as Coach

- **Prepare** the Learners
- **Meet** the Problem

- **Identify** What We Know, What We Need to Know, and Our Ideas
- **Define** the Problem Statement
- **Gather** and Share Information

Iterative

- **Generate** Possible Solutions
- **Determine** the Best Fit of Solutions
- **Present** the Solution (Performance Assessment)
- **Debrief** the Problem

EMBED INSTRUCTION AND ASSESSMENTS

Coaching Students

Adapted from Torp & Sage (1998), p. 34. © 1996 Illinois Mathematics and Science Academy, Center for Problem-Based Learning, Aurora, IL.

In this chapter, to highlight the PBL teaching and learning events, we use a particular PBL learning experience centered on overpopulation of mosquitoes in a suburban area. Although this problem was designed as a professional development immersion experience (Center for Problem-Based Learning, 1996c), middle school and high school classrooms have also used it. Most recently, the instructional experience has reflected the growing problem with Tiger mosquitoes in and around used tire dumps, as well as the problem with mosquitoes in the greater New York metropolitan area. We frame our problem around the learner's role and situation and an articulation of the problem statement that we believe will drive inquiry and generate solutions.

Role and Situation

In a fictitious county, Center County, the mosquito population has exploded. Center County Manager Richard Clarke alerts the Center County Mosquito Abatement Agency to the citizens' concerns. Learners assume the role of community members selected for a panel advising the Center County Mosquito Abatement Agency. These advisors have the tasks of generating varying theories about why the mosquitoes have become so prevalent and investigating potential solutions to the problem.

Anticipated Problem Statement
How can we, as members of the advisory panel, determine possible causes of the mosquito population problem and recommend possible solutions in such a way that we consider all the relevant factors—health, social, environmental, political, and financial?

Preparing the Learners

Goal: Support learners as they encounter problem-based learning.

Support for the learners may take different forms, depending on such variables as the age of the learners, their interests and background, and the nature of the problem. Consider how teachers supported some other PBL experiences. A primary grade teacher prepared her students for a PBL experience about growing healthy plants by setting up several plant experiments students could observe and discuss (like a celery stalk absorbing colored water), putting out books related to plants in the reading area, and practicing the KWL strategy with her students (What do I *know*? What do I *want* to know? What have I *learned*?).

Two middle school teachers who team-teach using PBL prepare their students each year through team building, critical thinking activities, and creativity exercises. Other teachers choose to conduct a simulation-type experience or a small-scale, problem-based experience with students (two or three hours and less ill-structured) before they begin a lengthier, more complex PBL experience.

One area to avoid when preparing students is teaching the content of the problem before starting. PBL is distinguished from other types of experiential education because students learn the content and skills *in the course of* solving the problem. The appropriate amount and type of preparation—whether touching on content or processes encountered in the problem—must be determined based on the needs and experiences of your learners and the standards that address learning expectations. Students who have encountered PBL several times may not need any specific preparation before meeting a problem.

To prepare for solving our mosquito problem—

- Learners reflect on a real problem they have addressed; as a small group, we brainstorm about the problem-solving process we use when we encounter problems.
- Learners watch a brief video clip from the movie *Apollo 13*, in which the astronauts encounter the problem of the explosion in the rocket's oxygen tank.

Meeting the Problem

Goals: Support learners as they develop a personal stake in the problem; motivate them to want to solve it.

Sometimes, to afford students this stake and motivation, we place them in a role other than that of student (e.g., engineer, consultant, or concerned citizen) so that they may engage in the problem authentically. Who would actually be concerned about this problem? Who would have something to gain or lose if the situation were resolved in a particular way?

We can design meeting the problem in a number of ways to engage or hook students. One way that our partner teachers and we often use is to give students an authentic-looking letter or document that describes their role in the problem. The document introduces the problem briefly and gives enough detail so that students can make an initial attempt at defining it.

Another way to introduce students to a problem is to identify or enlist someone who will ask the students to help solve a problem of personal concern, such as a principal asking primary grade students to help determine why plants are not growing well in her garden. (See Chapter 1 for more about this problem.) Teachers have also designed brief dramatic skits to introduce a problem; for example, two high school students may act out an argument that escalates into abuse to introduce middle school students (in their new roles as genetic consultants) to a problem relating to the possible genetic causes of aggression. A video clip, newspaper article, notices from a public agency, or phone message recording can also be used.

In the mosquito problem, the learners met the problem through a memo, shown in Figure 4.2.

Identifying What We Know, What We Need to Know, and Our Ideas

Goals

- *Support learners in developing an awareness of what they know and need to know, and what ideas they have about the problem.*
- *Activate learners' prior knowledge about the problem.*

- *Provide focus for preparing to gather information needed to solve the problem.*

This event allows learners to understand the problematic situation. Based on this understanding, students begin to investigate relevant subjects and eventually suggest how to bring the problem to an acceptable resolution. Teachers coach students to probe the knowledge they have from meeting the problem as well as from their experiences. Students document this information on a "know" chart or document. The "need to knows" are issues the students believe are critical to finding out more about the problem; students record this information also. The "need to knows" typically drive students' initial information-gathering efforts. Student "ideas" may relate to how to locate information, or to initial hunches they have about the cause of the problem or even possible solutions. This event is repeated as necessary as students continue to gather new information that may change what they know—and may raise new need-to-know questions and ideas. Figure 4.3 shows examples in the three goal areas for the mosquito problem.

Defining the Problem Statement

Goal: Support learners in (1) stating the overriding issue or problem in the circumstances they have encountered, and (2) identifying a subset of conflicting conditions that a good solution must serve.

For the problem statement, we often use the prompt, "How can we . . . in such a way that . . . ?" A question framed in this manner helps pull together the problem and the conditions under which students will solve it. As most of us know from our work (and personal) lives, attempting

---

FIGURE 4.2
Meet the Problem: Memo for the Mosquito Problem

Center County, Illinois
A Community with a Vision of the Future

Richard C. Clarke, County Manager

M * E * M * O

Date: July 10, 1997
To: Center County Mosquito Abatement Agency Staff
From: Richard C. Clarke
Subject: Increase in the Mosquito Population

As you can see from the attached newspaper item, residents of Center County are under siege from a population of mosquitoes—possibly the largest ever. The usual mosquito control methods seem to be ineffective in reducing this unprecedented outbreak. Determine the cause of this outbreak and recommend appropriate solutions. I will expect to hear from you on the afternoon of July 17, 1997. In the meantime, I will contact the state to obtain the necessary additional funds to implement the best solution.

Reprinted from Torp & Sage (1998), p. 37. *Source:* Center for Problem-Based Learning (1996c).

FIGURE 4.3
A Sample of What We Know, What We Need to Know, and Our Ideas About the Mosquito Problem

Know	Need to Know	Ideas
We need to find causes to mosquito problem in Center County. We must have solutions in a week. Mosquitoes can travel up to 30–40 miles. Rainfall was normal this year.	Geography of entire county. Are these mosquitoes indigenous to this area? Conditions that make mosquitoes thrive. Budget. Have drainage patterns changed recently?	Maybe there is a lot of standing water in the area. Maybe a natural occurrence (like fallen trees) has created standing water. The mosquitoes are resistant to current spraying through mutation or adaptation.

Reprinted from Torp & Sage (1998), p. 38.

to solve a problem is difficult unless we understand the problem and how much of it we can actually control.

The first problem statement from one group working on the mosquito problem was,

> How can we find a way to return the county's mosquito population to normal so that we do the following:
> - Consider environmental impact (livability, biodiversity, and populations).
> - Reduce health risks.

- Prevent the problem from happening again.
- Keep costs reasonable.

Conditions that contribute to a viable solution often conflict. A cost-effective insecticide may very well pose unacceptable health and environmental risks. Reducing health risks beyond a certain point may be impossible or beyond the financial means of the community.

The problem statement is revisited as students gather and share information that may change learners' understanding of the nature of the problem. For example, the group later revised the preceding problem statement to read: "How can we control the mosquito population in Center County. . . ?" This focus is quite different from "return the county's mosquito population to normal."

Learners may also map the problem as they understand more about it and develop hunches about the potential causes, solutions, and consequences. Figure 4.4 shows a map for the mosquito problem. This connective representation helps identify linkages and potential causal relationships that did not become evident in a more text-based approach.

Gathering and Sharing Information

Goals

- *Support learners in planning and implementing effective information-gathering, sharing, and meaning-making strategies.*
- *Support learners in understanding how new information contributes to understanding the problem, and how to*

FIGURE 4.4
One Possible Problem Map for the Mosquito Problem

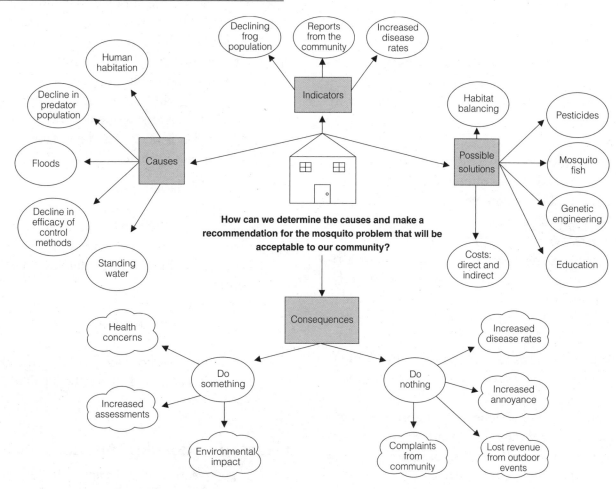

Reprinted from Torp & Sage (1998), p. 39. *Source:* Center for Problem-Based Learning (1996c).

evaluate information in light of its contribution to that understanding.

- *Support learners in interpersonal communication and collaborative learning, which contribute to effective problem solving.*

Learners typically work in collaborative groups of three to five, organized around particular "need to knows" that they have selected. When information gathering is complete, these topic groups are often "jigsawed" (new groups are formed with one person from each topic group, so each can share the gathered information). This part of PBL—which is one of the most critical steps—often takes the most time, depending on the problem's complexity, and probably requires the most sophisticated coaching and questioning skills from teachers. We want all students—no matter what aspect of the problem they personally may have investigated deeply—to come to a holistic understanding of the entire situation and the problem or problems embedded within it. Teachers usually determine that their goals at this stage are met when students are no longer finding pertinent, new information or when a deadline requires learners to solve the problem with whatever information they have at that point.

Two situations for which teachers should prepare themselves are students having difficulty locating any information, or finding such an abundance of information, much of it irrelevant, that they may initially struggle. For example, contacting experts on the telephone or asking for price in-

formation on plant fertilizer may be new experiences. Some learners may locate large amounts of information on the Internet, yet not be able to determine what information is most pertinent to the problem. Groups may argue internally over who should perform what tasks.

After several PBL experiences, teachers learn how to coach students through these difficulties, and students learn to assess themselves and their groups on how well they are gathering and sharing information. Maintaining a focus on the problem statement is helpful in determining what information is needed and most useful.

In the mosquito problem, learners

- Read and discuss information from the Internet on varieties of mosquitoes and different types of mosquito control that the agency can provide.
- Check local and state policies as presented in an agency brochure and a manual on state mosquito control.
- Determine whether other resources, such as conflicting viewpoints on the usefulness of biological controls, are accurate and pertinent.
- Ask questions about local conditions, such as population shifts and land use in the affected area.

Generating Possible Solutions

Goal: Support learners in articulating the full range *of possible options for addressing the problem they have defined.*

Again, going back to the problem statement, particularly the conditions for solving the problem, learners begin to recommend solutions based on the information they have gathered. One useful tool for organizing the possible solutions is a decision-making matrix. Figure 4.5 shows an excerpt from a matrix for the mosquito problem.

Determining the Solutions That Fit Best

Goal: Support learners in using the benchmarks of good thinking to evaluate the benefits and consequences of each solution.

The students' goal is to create the most acceptable set of outcomes in response to the conditions specified in the problem statement. This event is crucial to producing a well-supported and feasible solution. Critical thinking literature (for example, see Lipman [1988], Norris [1985]) supports the fact that skillful, responsible thinking comes about from good judgment supported by criteria, context, self-correction, and explicit reasons for drawing a conclusion. Students have to balance needs and risks, assess the feasibility of options, and consider which solution moves them closer to their idealized solution.

In the mosquito problem, learners evaluated several possible solutions, including education, chemical application, and further research. A particular group determined that the approach that fit best for the problem was a combination of these three solutions.

FIGURE 4.5
Excerpt from a Decision-Making Matrix for the Mosquito Problem

Strategy	Pros	Cons	Consequences
Education Free public service announcement. Speak to community groups. Press releases. Content: health issues/risk, prevention, comfort, current treatment.	Low cost. Additional state funds available. Donations. Informed citizens. Lifesaving.	People may think the agency is not doing enough. Fear? Lack of interest?	Change people's minds and behavior. Potentially help reduce mosquito problem. Breeds tolerance and understanding of the bigger ecosystem picture.
Chemical Application	Additional state funds available. Donation.	High cost. Safety?	**?**

Reprinted from Torp & Sage (1998), p. 41.

Presenting the Solution (Performance Assessment)

Goal: Support learners in effectively articulating and demonstrating what they know, how they know it, and why and for whom knowing is important.

Teachers often arrange for outside experts whom students have consulted or others knowledgeable about the problem issues to serve on a panel to assess the recommendations and challenge assumptions when students present their solutions. For example, in a middle school problem about a prairie on the school campus that was restored yet not being maintained properly, the panel consisted of the original landscape architect, district maintenance and grounds personnel, the district business manager, a local environmentalist, and a school board member. A typical format is that several groups from the class present solutions (often very different), and the panel members question each group after its presentation. Assessing this culminating performance is usually conducted using a detailed rubric—often codeveloped by the teacher and students—on content, presentation skills, teamwork, and fit of solution.

As we have observed, much student learning occurs here. Learners hear another group giving details or reasons they had not considered, or offering incorrect information. Panel members ask questions for which students may not be prepared in initial PBL experiences. Through these challenges, students learn how to present more thoroughly thought-out and well-supported solutions, and to consider the perspective of other stakeholders or their audience in what information is most important. Students become adept at developing visuals to accompany their presentation and in explaining why they are presenting their particular solution.

In the mosquito problem, learners in four working groups presented their solution to a representative of the county manager (who had asked them to work on the problem). Peer groups used common criteria to assess solutions and presentations. The groups' solution read as follows:

> We find the best solution to be a combination of education, chemical application, and research. Education is the least expensive and perhaps most effective alternative to prevent more problems, reassure area citizens, and make them aware of the agency's current policies and treatments. Limited chemical application, in this crisis situation, is also appropriate, using additional state funding available. Finally, we support further research by agency staff to determine why this outbreak of nonfloodwater mosquitoes is occurring at this time.

Although presentations, poster sessions, and reports offer rich opportunities to evaluate student learning, we also advocate ongoing embedded assessments (see Chapter 7). These periodic, in-process assessments can take many forms—such as status reports, responses to phone messages from problem stakeholders, mind maps, and problem statements. Whatever forms are used, they provide valuable snapshots of learning that can inform midcourse corrections and diagnose difficulties that students are encountering with the PBL experience.

Debriefing the Problem

Goal: For learners to reflect together on what they have learned and to place new learning within a cognitive framework of knowing.

Learners review the effectiveness of the strategies they used and consider what they might do differently in another problem situation. They discuss issues still unresolved or open to further investigation. Sometimes follow-up, particularly in a problem actually occurring in the community, will occur until other stakeholders have resolved the issues. These cognitive and metacognitive strategies—thinking, and thinking about our own learning—are important not only for adhering to benchmarks of good thinking, but also for providing a sense of completion to learners who have become personally invested in the problem. They need a realistic awareness of the effect their recommended solutions will have in resolving the problem.

In addition, because these experiences embody essential standards-based learning outcomes, we must help students raise that learning to a conscious level, place it within the field or discipline of knowing, and understand through conceptual threads the connectedness among these fields. Students frequently enjoy PBL experiences so much that they disconnect them from any type of learning experience. Explicitly making these connections is essential. *PBL is not a timeout from school or learning: PBL is authentic learning at school.*

For debriefing the mosquito problem, we had a whole-group discussion in which we discussed the entire PBL experience and what students had learned about themselves as learners. We also designed a journal entry. Figure 4.6 is a sample journal entry showing learners' responses.

Summary

Through the teaching and learning events in PBL, students construct knowledge revolving around a relevant problematic situation in a rigorous, thoughtful, connected way. We agree with Savery and Duffy (1995): PBL exemplifies a constructivist model for education, which serves to best prepare our students for life now and in the future. In the next chapter, we help you begin to develop your own PBL curriculum.

FIGURE 4.6
Journal Entry for Debriefing the Mosquito Problem

---

1. *Describe your response to this problem as a learner. What were you thinking, feeling, and valuing?*
   - I found it interesting having to find a solution to a complex problem with limited and sometimes contradictory information and with not very much time (real life).

   - I was thinking of the importance of the information you receive in defining the strategy for attacking a problem.

   - I learned a lot about the different kinds of mosquitoes and how they attack and where they live. The different ways communities try to handle the problems. The disregard that we have as humans for nature around us, and what we do may have a much larger impact than we are aware of.

   - Much, much more engaged in this situation and more willing to learn. Very interesting method of teaching here!

2. *What questions or puzzles remain?*
   - If this problem were real, would my thought pattern have been the same? How many more problems come from one seemingly simple problem?

Reprinted from Torp & Sage (1998), p. 43.

5

How Do You Design a Problem-Based Learning Curriculum?

NOW THAT YOU HAVE A SENSE OF HOW A PBL EVENT PLAYS out in a classroom, we'll step back and consider how to design a PBL experience for your students.

In any design activity, we need clarity about the essential elements that are available to us. What's on our palette? A friend who is a successful landscape designer sees plant materials as representing varying colors, textures, and forms. She blends these components into a coherent design, varying one or more, but always conscious of the interplay and balance among the three elements. As we design PBL experiences, we must be aware of our three essential elements—context, students, and curriculum—and the interrelationship among them that contributes to coherent, holistic learning experiences. Where do we begin?

Thinking About Context

Many times in curriculum design and development we start with the knowledge, skills, and dispositions we believe our students should, respectively, know, be able to do, and value. Through task analysis and from our experience, we piece together what we consider to be a holistic and connected lesson or unit. In doing so, we often miss the relationships and connections that provide coherence and relevance for our students who must engage with the learning experience. For example, in designing a unit around tropical rain forests, beginning with the flora and fauna and leading up to their effect upon global environmental issues, we might overlook connections to the local culture, the economic development of the region, or society's role in their destruction. As educators, we tend to assume students will "see" complex interrelationships when, for the most part, they don't.

In designing a problem-based learning experience, we begin instead with the problematic situation—a fully integrated whole—and tease out the knowledge, skills, dispositions, and standards-based learning opportunities that the authentic context of the problem exposes. Many times we have heard Grant Wiggins speak of "content as the means to performance ends" as he points out the need for evidence of understanding. PBL experiences expose rich content and skills and place students in situations where they can interact with both the people and products authentic to that situation. Students go beyond knowing to understanding as they move across contexts and situations, adapting, coping, and thinking deeply. "That's why PBL is such an elegant piece of design" (Wiggins & Jacobs, 1995).

Thinking About Students

As we design in-context curriculum, we are compelled to carefully consider students' learning characteristics and interests. What makes students unique as a group or as individuals? We encourage you to make a list of your learners' characteristics and add to it periodically. One middle grade teacher began by thinking about her students' knowledge, skills, developmental level, and dispositions, and generated the following list:

- Want to be independent—yet can be childlike and develop hero worship.
- Criticize society.
- Are ready to refine reasoning skills and understand abstract concepts.
- Can be self-conscious about new tasks.
- Care deeply about their personal situation and want to fit in with peer group.

A high school teacher at an alternative school began with this list:

- Rebel against traditional teaching methods.
- Perceive school as an alternative to prison.
- Have experienced a large measure of failure.
- Cannot see a practical application for what is taught in school.
- Value real experiences.

Thinking About Curriculum

Before designing a PBL experience, we need to develop a set of priorities for our teaching. Consider the outcomes for any unit or course and the learning standards to target. What are some conceptual, skill-based, and dispositional outcomes that you and your school value highly enough and to which you would invest instructional time? One middle grade teacher in Illinois prepared the following list of outcomes. We have added references to appropriate Illinois Learning Standards to highlight the rich, standards-based learning opportunities targeted (Illinois State Board of Education, 1997):

- ***Understand such issues as biodiversity and economic impacts.***

    Illinois Science Goal 12: Understand the fundamental concepts, principles, and interconnections of the life, physical, and earth/space sciences.

    Standard B. Know and apply concepts that describe how living things interact with each other and with their environment.

- ***Design and conduct experiments.***

    Illinois Science Goal 13: Understand the fundamental concepts, principles, and interconnections of the life, physical, and earth/space sciences.

    Standard A. Know and apply the accepted practices of science.

- ***Use graphs to illustrate probability and interpret data.***

    Illinois Math Goal 10: Collect, organize, and analyze data using statistical methods; predict results; and interpret uncertainty using concepts of probability.

    Standard A. Organize, describe, and make predictions from existing data.

    Standard B. Formulate questions, design data collection methods, gather and analyze data, and communicate findings.

    Standard C. Determine, describe, and apply the probabilities of events.

- ***Communicate effectively with a given audience.***

    Illinois Language Arts Goal 3: Write to communicate for a variety of purposes.

    Standard A. Use correct grammar, spelling, punctuation, capitalization, and structure.

    Standard B. Compose well-organized and coherent writing for specific purposes and audiences.

    Standard C. Communicate ideas in writing to accomplish a variety of purposes.

- ***Develop self-directed learning strategies.***

    The Illinois Applications of Learning address applied learning skills that cross academic disciplines and reinforce the important learning of these disciplines. Using these skills influences students' success in school, in the workplace, and beyond. Solving problems is one of these integrative aspects of learning that intersects and has meaning for each academic discipline.

    Solving Problems. Recognize and investigate problems; formulate and propose solutions supported by reason and evidence.

- ***Appreciate the views and contributions of others.***

    Illinois Social Science Goal 14: Understand political systems, with an emphasis on the United States. Through the study of various forms and levels of and the documents and institutions of the United States government, students will develop the skills and knowledge that they need to be contributing citizens, now and in the future.

(A Mosquito Abatement District, referenced in Chapter 4, is one such political entity.)

Standard A. Understand and explain basic principles of the United States government.

Standard B. Understand the structures and functions of the political systems of Illinois, the United States, and other nations.

Standard C. Understand election processes and responsibilities of citizens.

Standard D. Understand the roles and influences of individuals and interest groups in the political systems of Illinois, the United States, and other nations.

14.D.5 Interpret a variety of public policies and issues from the perspectives of different individuals and groups.

Illinois Language Arts Goal 5: Use the language arts to acquire, assess, and communicate information.

Standard A. Locate, organize, and use information from various sources to answer questions, solve problems, and communicate ideas.

A high school teacher in an integrated health occupations program included the following outcomes; state or local standards apply on many levels to such a list:

- Culture and identify microorganisms.
- Differentiate between "normal" and "diseased" human body states.

- Describe how a catalyst affects a rate of reaction.
- Explore several methods of chemical analysis.
- Develop library skills.
- Use the Internet as a research source.

By explicitly exposing what we already know about the essential elements of context, students, and curriculum, we are better able to blend and balance their contribution to each element of the design of PBL curriculum as it begins to meld into implementation.

We see most effective PBL units unfolding quite naturally through the design component and the decisions that teacher-designers make as they choose a relevant problem, develop the unit around this problem, and build their teaching and learning template. Teacher-coaches then implement their plans through a coaching strategy as students meet, investigate, and attempt to resolve their ill-structured problem. Figure 5.1 (which expands on Figure 2.2) presents our conception of how a PBL unit flows from idea to actuality.

Generating and Playing with Ideas

Increasingly, teachers are challenged to provide sufficient coverage. On the one hand, they must cover an increasing volume of curriculum; on the other hand, analysts call for covering the curriculum in more depth. One way to deal with this problem is to shift perspective and play with ideas. You may not normally think of play when organizing curriculum and planning for instruction, but *intellectual* play

FIGURE 5.1
The Flow of a PBL Unit

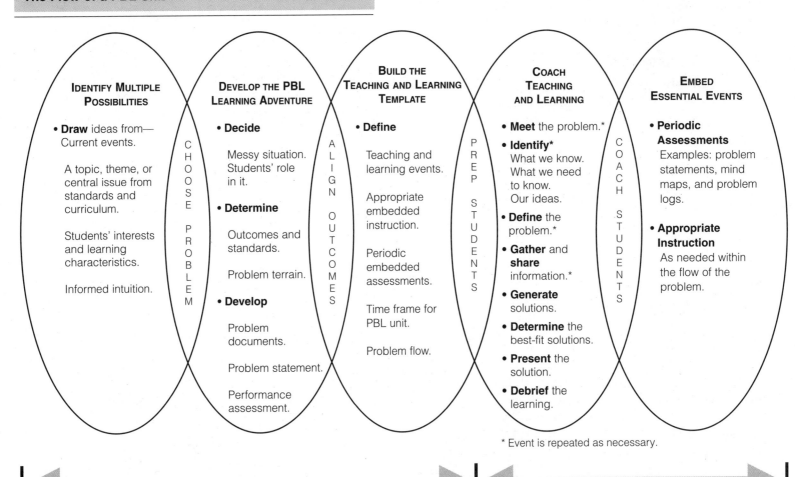

IDENTIFY MULTIPLE POSSIBILITIES

- **Draw** ideas from—
  Current events.

  A topic, theme, or central issue from standards and curriculum.

  Students' interests and learning characteristics.

  Informed intuition.

CHOOSE PROBLEM

DEVELOP THE PBL LEARNING ADVENTURE

- **Decide**

  Messy situation. Students' role in it.

- **Determine**

  Outcomes and standards.

  Problem terrain.

- **Develop**

  Problem documents.

  Problem statement.

  Performance assessment.

ALIGN OUTCOMES

BUILD THE TEACHING AND LEARNING TEMPLATE

- **Define**

  Teaching and learning events.

  Appropriate embedded instruction.

  Periodic embedded assessments.

  Time frame for PBL unit.

  Problem flow.

PREP STUDENTS

COACH TEACHING AND LEARNING

- **Meet** the problem.*
- **Identify***
  What we know. What we need to know. Our ideas.
- **Define** the problem.*
- **Gather** and **share** information.*
- **Generate** solutions.
- **Determine** the best-fit solutions.
- **Present** the solution.
- **Debrief** the learning.

COACH STUDENTS

EMBED ESSENTIAL EVENTS

- **Periodic Assessments**
  Examples: problem statements, mind maps, and problem logs.

- **Appropriate Instruction**
  As needed within the flow of the problem.

* Event is repeated as necessary.

Problem Design

Problem Implementation

Adapted from Torp & Sage (1998), p. 47. © 1996 Illinois Mathematics and Science Academy, Center for Problem-Based Learning, Aurora, IL.

enables us to deal with new ideas, consider what's possible, and identify what's missing (Doll, 1993). Figure 5.2 shows the overlapping nature of elements to be considered.

Recently, we worked with a group of 16 Illinois educators whose goals centered on integrating PBL and the scientific literacy habits of mind identified by the Illinois State Board of Education (Illinois State Board of Education's Center for Scientific Literacy, 1994). Figure 5.3 summarizes these habits of mind.

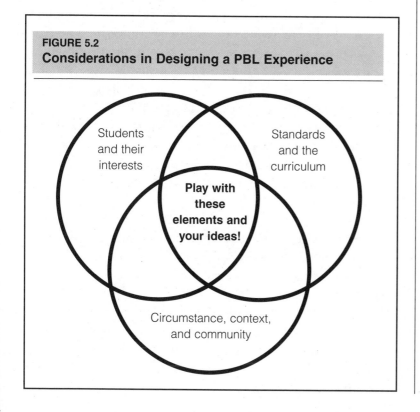

FIGURE 5.2
Considerations in Designing a PBL Experience

Students and their interests

Standards and the curriculum

Play with these elements and your ideas!

Circumstance, context, and community

FIGURE 5.3
Scientific Literacy Habits of Mind

A capacity to question, comprehend, interpret, and make inferences.

An ability to communicate mathematically and scientifically.

An awareness that the nature of science and mathematics is ongoing, evolving, and refined through investigation.

An appreciation of the interdependence and interrelatedness of science, mathematics, and technology.

An understanding of the strengths and limitations of science, mathematics, and technology in our complex world.

Reprinted from Torp & Sage (1998), p. 48. *Source:* Illinois State Board of Education's Center for Scientific Literacy (1994), p. 1.

We played with several idea "umbrellas" as we began the PBL design process to develop a program for middle grade students—with a goal of improving their scientific literacy. Presented here are the beginnings of some messy, ill-structured problems. What opportunities do you see to cover several goals and ignite student interest under a single umbrella?

Building Another Bridge to Accommodate Increasing Traffic

The Fox Valley area is growing steadily. Traffic is increasing, and a new bridge across the Fox River is needed. Several sites have been proposed, but each one has opposition. One site crosses a forest preserve that contains rare plant and animal species. Other sites concern homeowners who want the bridge built somewhere else. Is the bridge really needed? At which site should it be built? Who decides?

Underage Smoking in the Community

Underage smoking is on the rise in the school district. Beyond the obvious addiction problem and dangerous health risks to the children, additional concerns have surfaced. Cigarettes are a discipline problem in the middle school and seem to prompt rebellious behavior. Several students have turned to stealing the money they need for cigarettes. What, if anything, should the middle school do about student smoking?

Declining Frog Populations in the County

The middle school backs up to wetlands that contain a wide variety of unusual and interesting plants and animals. Science classes have used this area for years to collect and study plants and animals. Lately, students and teachers have noticed a dramatic decrease in the frog population. Finding frogs at all is hard. What happened to all the frogs?

Look to your community for current issues and consider opening some umbrellas of your own. Newspapers, weekly news magazines, talk radio, town council and park board meetings, and the Internet may help seed your thinking. Figure 5.4 shows sample problematic situations some teachers have used.

Mapping the Terrain of Problem Possibilities

Working from a bank of possibilities like these umbrella ideas, visualize each topic in some way and map out the terrain of problem ideas and connections. An upper elementary teacher mapped out or webbed several other idea possibilities that interested her because of learner appeal, integrative curricular yield, and real-world connections. Figure 5.5 shows three map skeletons as she added topics and details related to her central ideas.

Mapping is an invaluable tool with multiple applications for PBL. Figure 5.6 details how we have used maps.

Once you can see and examine the terrain of these possibilities, look for areas of conflict or dissonance. What is unacceptable in each situation? Are political, social, or interpersonal conflicts apparent? Do inequities of the treatment, support, resources, or results surface? What pulls you in, sparks a need-to-know, and begs for resolution? Do multiple stakeholders have a vested interest in this problem? One teacher contends that with messy, ill-structured problems, any solution that students propose "is going to be controversial to one person or another. That's just part of problem solving." We look also for situations that have multiple solutions. Most problems—especially real-world problems—rarely have one right answer.

Select a problematic center for your PBL experience that maximizes both engagement and learning. Two middle school teachers, Louise and Karoline, grapple with the issues of motivation and curricular payoff in a brief question-and-answer interchange about restoring a prairie adjacent to their school:

FIGURE 5.4
Samples of Problematic Situations

Problematic Situations "Attract"

Charge innate curiosity with a "needs-to-be-solved" pull.

Students are advisors to a state representative who must vote on a bill to regulate livestock waste management just as a "mega" hog farm is proposed for the county. *What environmental, economic, political, and societal consequences should be considered?*

—Deb Gerdes, 6th grade language arts teacher, Knoxville, IL

Primary students are intrigued by a playground rumor of an alligator in the sewer. *Could the rumor be true, and what should they do if they find out that it is?*

—Karen Jensen, primary grade teacher, Aurora, IL

What is it that
- **Inspires?**
- **Intrigues?**
- **Informs?**

Problems surround students with issues, concerns, and puzzles—luring them inside the situation and propelling them toward action that's grounded in a true desire to learn and apply essential knowledge and skills to serve the needs of their problem.

Students are field agents for the Centers for Disease Control. They are asked to prepare a press release concerning plague patterns, conditions, and precautions based on 10 years of data. *What are the facts, who is the public, and how do we communicate effectively with them?*

—Bernard C. Hollister, American Studies teacher, Illinois Math and Science Academy (IMSA)

FIGURE 5.5
Maps of Possibility

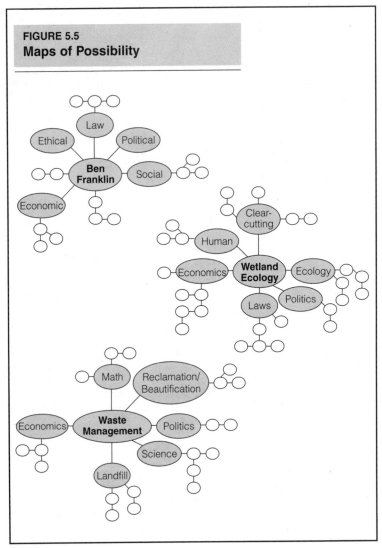

Reprinted from Torp & Sage (1998), p. 49. *Source:* Center for Problem-Based Learning (1996a).

FIGURE 5.6
Using Maps to Make Thinking Visible

Mind mapping is one way to record thinking visually so that it can be reviewed, organized, and refined. Several types can be used:

Maps of possibility. You can select and focus a problem by mapping the terrain of the topic and what you want a problem to accomplish.

Anticipated problem maps. You can map the actual components that present themselves in a given problem. These maps can help you plan for necessary resources by anticipating how students might make their way through a problem.

Curriculum maps. You can map the curricular connections within a given problem. These maps can help you identify key curricular outcomes for assessment and reporting.

Problem maps. Students can map the problem space to see the scope and connections within a problematic situation. These maps can help students generate ideas about needed resources or information and develop hypotheses about potential solutions.

Teachers can assess student learning by examining changes in students' actual maps of the problem throughout the teaching and learning process and by comparing students' final maps of the problem with maps generated by experts in the field of inquiry.

Reprinted from Torp & Sage (1998), p. 51.

Louise: What are we actually trying to do? I mean, are we trying to get them to show the rest of the students how they can save prairies in general?

Karoline: Yes, but I think we also want them to make a connection. I mean, they could learn all they want to about this prairie, but if . . . we don't get them to hook the rest of the school population into why we care about a prairie, then I think they are going to feel almost used.

They have chosen a problem that exposes rich content, but will their students care enough about saving and restoring the prairie adjacent to the school? Will students feel empowered to have meaningful input into the resolution? These connections are essential if learners are to delve into the complexity of the situation and move toward action.

Planning a Problem-Based Learning Adventure

More than one student has commented that PBL is a learning adventure. With any journey, though, travel along the right route requires planning and preparation. We're not talking about planning for instruction and the details of day-to-day implementation (see Chapters 4 and 6), but rather the overall sense of knowing where you're going, how you're going to get there, and what you'll need to do once you've arrived. This work sounds much more linear than it really is; actually, the activities of planning a problem-based learning adventure are so interrelated that they evolve together:

- Identify learning outcomes and connections to learning standards.
- Decide on a problematic situation and students' roles in that situation.
- Figure out how students will meet the problem.
- Develop the anticipated problem statement.
- Describe the performance of understanding.
- Gather information.

More and more, as we continue to design a PBL learning experience, we need to put ourselves in our learners' places and anticipate their questions, thinking, needs, and responses to the ambiguity and complexity of ill-structured problems. In this way, we begin to plan for their PBL learning adventure. Figure 5.7 charts a course and identifies critical milestones in this planning process.

Knowing Where You're Going

Two important planning activities help frame the students' learning adventure:

- Identifying the learning outcomes that the problem exposes.
- Describing the performance of understanding in which learners will engage as an authentic companion to their investigation.

Identify Learning Outcomes and Connections to Learning Standards. Once we have chosen the problematic topic around which our PBL experience will revolve, we identify

FIGURE 5.7
Planning a Problem-Based Learning Adventure

 Before taking to the road, consider your destination and choose or define outcomes worthy of your effort, students' investment, and the curriculum.

How will students meet the messy situation that contains the problem needing resolution?

- How are the boundaries of the problem space determined?

- What alerts students to their **role** and **situation**?

- Is it a document, a drama, or ??

How will students make the journey?

- What **role** will capture students' interest and provide a platform for making a contribution to problem resolution?

- What messy **situation** will draw students into its depths without broadcasting the root problem, foreshadowing the solution, or providing too much information?

Remember . . .

Getting where you want to go requires planning and preparation!

How will students define the root problem?

- How will you create the scenario and organize the information so that students will get to the essential issue and critical conditions of the problem?

- Knowing what you know about your students and the problematic scenario, how do you think students will define the root problem?

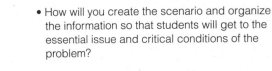

How will students show that they have arrived at their destination?

What meaningful **performance assessment** will afford students the opportunity to interact with real stakeholders of this problem **and** show what they have learned in an integrated and authentic way?

the learning outcomes to serve as our beacon while we investigate the problem. Extending a map of possibility into a curriculum map is one method. By examining concepts, skills, and processes exposed through mapping, teachers make explicit connections to curriculum by adding to their maps direct curricular references at the perimeter. Figure 5.8 shows this connection by a document shape with the upper right corner turned down. The figure is a curriculum map that a team of teachers conceptualized to use as PBL curriculum for IMSA's Summer Challenge Program for middle school students. These students, as consultants for a local mayor, needed to determine the best possible location for a new municipal landfill. Such a problem exposes rich content in multiple subject areas.

A planning team for a different program, the Illinois Problem-Based Learning Network (IPBLN)—addressing a problem of tobacco use among middle school students—chose to categorize and list learning outcomes exposed through the mapping process, as shown in Figure 5.9. The outcomes emerged from the major program goals related to content, self-directed learning, thinking and reasoning, and team collaboration (see Figure 5.10).

Describe the Performance of Understanding. What meaningful performance assessment will allow students to interact with the problem's real stakeholders and show what students have learned in an integrated and authentic way? (Chapter 7 addresses assessment possibilities.) To resolve this question, we encourage teachers to think carefully about the problem and select an assessment that is authentic to the situation. In reality, this decision is not something we can determine until we are clear about the role that students will take on as they immerse themselves in the problem.

Knowing How You're Going to Get There

Once you know where you are going, you'll need to consider how you and your students will travel through the twists and turns of the problem. We have found that before developing a more detailed teaching and learning template (see Chapter 4), you must carry out the following tasks:

- Decide on a problematic situation and students' roles in that situation.
- Figure out how students will meet the problem.
- Develop the anticipated problem statement.
- Gather relevant information.

As we stated in the previous section, even though these actions are presented in a seemingly linear fashion, in reality, they evolve together. Gathering relevant information from experts or local contacts will more than likely inform the selection of a role and situation. The interrelatedness of these planning actions cannot be stressed enough.

Decide on a Problematic Situation and Students' Role in That Situation. As mentioned earlier, ill-structured problems present a challenge for many different stakeholders. If we examine the issue of landfill site selection in a suburban area (see earlier discussion on site selection and Figure 5.8), we can identify many individuals who might have

FIGURE 5.8
Curriculum Map for the Landfill Problem

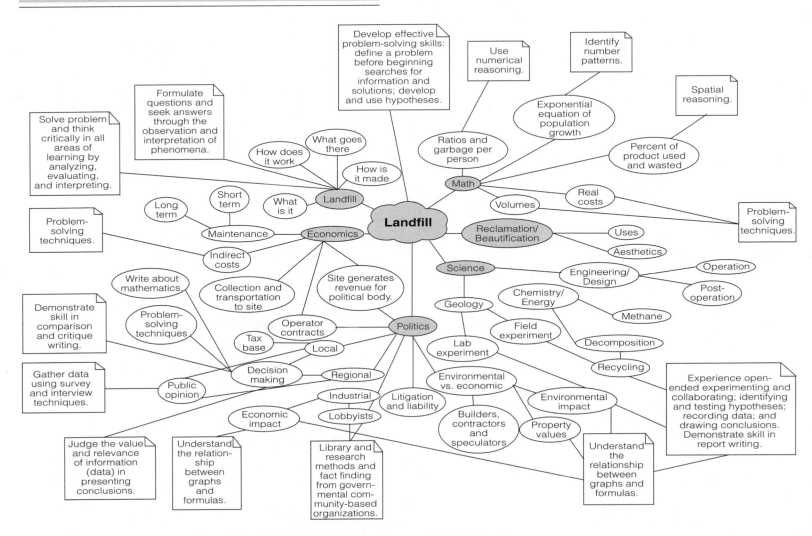

Reprinted from Torp & Sage (1998), p. 53. *Source:* Adapted from Finkle, Briggs, Hinton, Thompson, & Dods (1994).

FIGURE 5.9
Map of Possibility for the Tobacco Use Problem

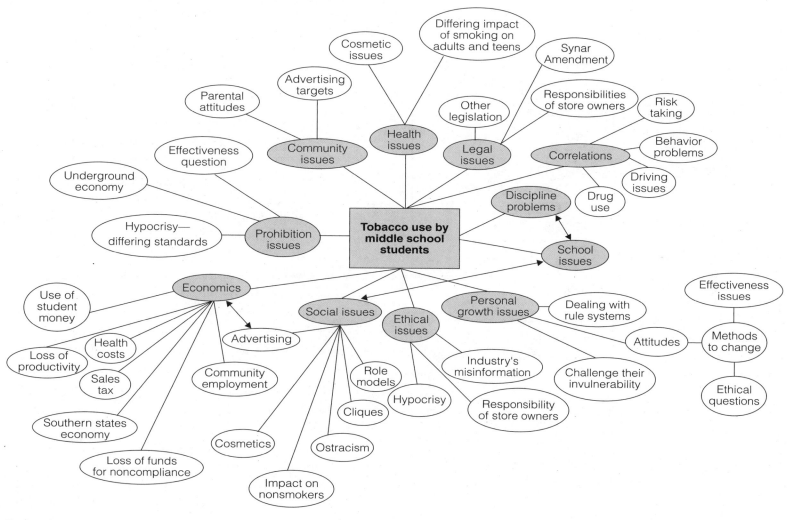

Reprinted from Torp & Sage (1998), p. 56. *Source:* Illinois Problem-Based Learning Network (1996).

FIGURE 5.10
Learning Outcomes for the Tobacco Use Problem

Content

Examine tobacco use choices and consequences for teenagers.

Review legal and social issues related to tobacco use among teenagers.

Consider health, ethical, and economic issues involving tobacco.

Analyze sources of tobacco research and information.

Know background information about the tobacco industry.

Self-Directed Learning

Develop assertiveness skills.

Identify relevant and reliable materials.

Utilize effective communication skills.

Develop personal responsibility.

Make choices based on evidence.

Thinking and Reasoning

Generate questions that focus and direct inquiry.

Analyze data from multiple sources.

Read, interpret, and transform data from graphs and charts.

Compare and contrast varied perspectives.

Develop critical thinking and decision-making skills.

Synthesize information.

Team Collaboration

Engage in healthy interactions with peers, adults, and community.

Provide efficient and effective help and assistance to each other.

Exchange needed resources with team.

Encourage achievement of goals.

Reprinted from Torp & Sage (1998), p. 57. *Source:* Adapted from Illinois Problem-Based Learning Network (1996).

a vested interest in the problem and potential solutions—local politicians, homeowners whose property values are at risk, environmentalists, corporate officials of the landfill management group, taxpayers, transportation department officials, soil and water district scientists, and so on.

Our challenge is to select a role in which the students will gain a full understanding of the problem and its complexity. We want them to consider the central issue and not simply address the concerns of one set of stakeholders. We also want them to step into a role that will interest them and provide them with a sense of empowerment in the situation. In the landfill problem as developed for upper middle school students, the designers placed students in the role of environmental engineers employed by a consulting firm. The firm had been hired to advise the mayor of a local community about the viability of three potential sites.

We need to stress the importance, once again, of playing with several possibilities. The choice of role and situation is critical in design. An upper elementary grade teacher tested a variety of possibilities before making her selection. Figure 5.11 shows the roles she was considering placing students in to engage the problem of wetlands development. In this problem, an oil company was seeking to purchase drilling rights within a protected wetland habitat for migrating birds.

Asking herself, "What if the central issue is . . . and the role is . . . and the final performance would logically be to . . . ?" she was able to select a role and situation appropriate for her students, where they would need to consider varying stakeholder positions. She then created an anticipated

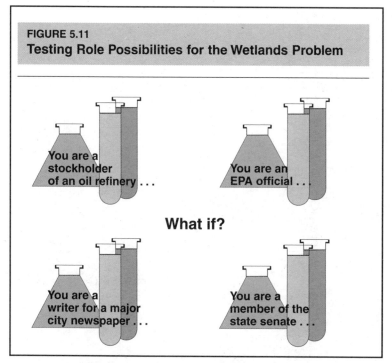

FIGURE 5.11
Testing Role Possibilities for the Wetlands Problem

You are a stockholder of an oil refinery . . .

You are an EPA official . . .

What if?

You are a writer for a major city newspaper . . .

You are a member of the state senate . . .

Reprinted from Torp & Sage (1998), p. 57. *Source:* Adapted from Vitale-Ortlund (1994).

cepts according to the demands of the role and situation with which you are working. You will see how problems can change significantly.

Another important consideration is the scope of the chosen role. If the problem and role are relatively narrow, the problem experience is more contained. For example, students may grapple with a problem that involves a personal relationship, an individual's decision-making struggle, or a problem involving the student and a peer group. A problem and role, on the other hand, that are more global and that involve more stakeholders are more complex and deserve more time and other resources. These latter types of problems might engage students as they play the role of legislators considering the passage of a particular bill, stockholders assessing the merits of a merger or acquisition, or members of the scientific community weighing the ethical issues related to the use or misuse of new and controversial technology. In considering a personal and a more global approach, we recognize the infinite possibilities that occupy the middle ground.

Emphasizing the value of roles within a problem inquiry is an important step. Roles situated within the problem scenario enable students and teachers alike to step outside the constraints of familiar roles and become coinvestigators in the problem inquiry. They can be scientists, homeowners, police—anyone.

Another benefit of roles is that they personalize learning and give students ownership of the problem. In their position as stakeholders in the problem, students become immersed in the situation. They are situated in the center

problem map that reflected the role and situation she chose and played out the problem as she thought students might (see Figure 5.12). Seeing the curricular richness exposed through mapping, she identified state learning goals or outcomes relevant for her 4th and 5th grade students, adding such references to her map in the form of documents with a turned-down corner.

You may wish to map out different possibilities for the role and situation—highlighting, adding, and deleting con-

FIGURE 5.12
Anticipated Problem Map for the Wetlands Problem

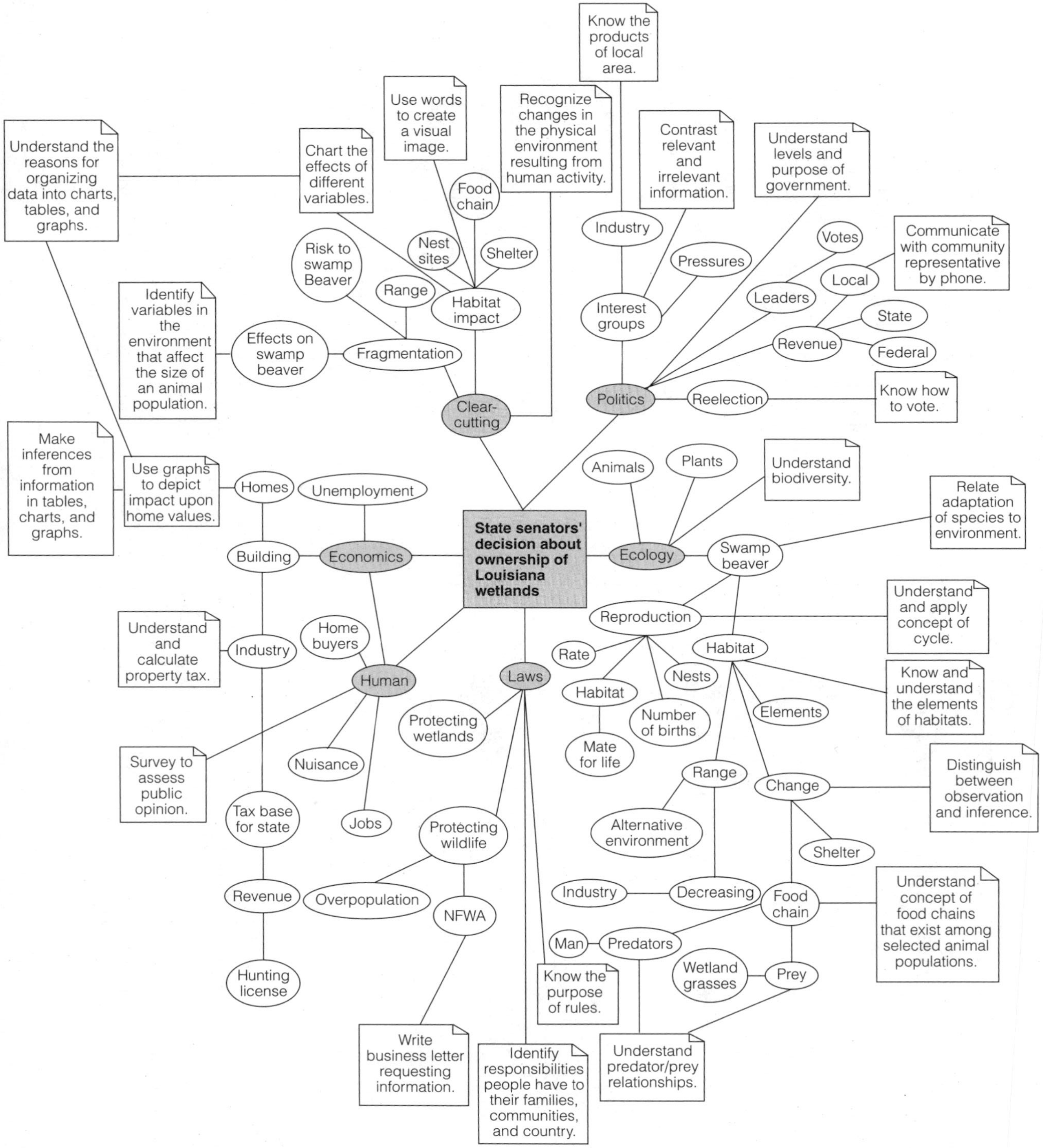

Reprinted from Torp & Sage (1998), p. 59. *Source:* Adapted from Vitale-Ortlund (1994).

of the learning experience rather than on the perimeter. Dorothy Heathcote (Heathcote & Herbert, 1980) contrasts these two perspectives as learning about things that are "here" or learning about things that are "there." "Here" is much more immediate and engaging, leading to deeper understanding. The student must take a stand on an issue, such as underage smoking, building a bridge, or planning a sanitary landfill.

We don't intend to imply that students should always assume a role outside of their own experience. If the problematic situation is one in which students would naturally own the problem, then keeping their perspective and their natural empathic connection as students makes sense. In this type of situation, we also want to make sure that students have a voice in resolving the problem. Several schools have used the issue of how to renovate a school or construct a new school. In most cases, students had an opportunity to present their recommendations to the school board, meet with the architect or building design team, and actually see some of their suggestions incorporated into the school's design. Giving students these opportunities assures that the PBL adventure transports them from empathy to advocacy and possible action (Newmann, 1990).

Figure Out How Students Will Meet the Problem. How will students meet the messy situation that contains the root problem needing resolution: a document, a phone message, a video clip, or a dramatization? Are these artifacts authentic or simulated? Remember the TV series "Mission Impossible"? Jim and the team listened to a short audiotape overviewing the situation and reviewed a dossier of pertinent materials. If you can find something that will self-destruct in 10 seconds, you'll certainly have the students' attention!

Many teachers are surprised at the power of authentic-looking documents as hooks to capture student interest and frame the PBL adventure. To continue with the landfill site selection example cited earlier in the chapter, students received simulated letters from varying stakeholders in the problem. A letter like the one shown in Figure 5.13, coupled with the staging of a staff meeting between Dr. Pace's representative (the teacher-coach) and her staff of environmental engineers (the students), serves to engage students and initiate their problem inquiry.

A first-rate introduction to a problem gives learners a sense of their stake and role in the problem and just enough information to launch their inquiry. Too much information may kill the desire to know more; too little can shut down the learners' attempts to get started.

Develop the Anticipated Problem Statement. Picture the circus performer who balances plates on the tips of reeds and spins them, trying to have as many plates as possible spinning at once. In designing a problem, sometimes we, too, need to keep a few plates spinning, such as when we are determining the problematic situation, students' roles, and problem engagement. Although we are presenting these design features here linearly, they are really defined and refined in concert. Given the stakeholder role and problematic situation you decide upon, as well as how the students meet the problematic scenario, you'll need to

---

FIGURE 5.13
Meet the Problem: Letter for the Landfill Problem

Village of Gotham
22 South First Street
Gotham, IL 60134   Walter R. Powers, Mayor

October 3, 1997

Dr. Michele Barron Pace
Prairie Environmental Services
1500 West Sullivan Road
Aurora, IL 60506-1000

Dear Dr. Pace:

This letter is to notify you that the Village of Gotham wishes to contract the services of your company to determine the feasibility of utilizing one of the available sites for a new landfill. This site is to replace our current Settler's Hill site, which is rapidly approaching capacity.

The sites, all owned by Cane County and therefore immediately available, are identified on the enclosed map as Gotham East, Gotham West, and Nelson Lake West.

I believe all other aspects of our solid waste disposal plan are effective and operating successfully.

Sincerely,

Walter R. Powers, Mayor

Reprinted from Torp & Sage (1998), p. 60. *Source:* Adapted from Finkle, Briggs, Hinton, Thompson, & Dods (1994).

anticipate what the students might identify as the real or root problem. In other words, as designer, you anticipate the stakeholder's perspective and context.

Your anticipated problem statement is the key feature to help you shape the design elements into a coherent plan for instruction. All the teacher's planning and all the students' learning are focused and guided by a clear statement of the problem. From our experience, successful problem statements have two essential parts:

- A statement of the central issue of the problem.
- The identification of conditions that will signal an acceptable solution.

We often use the following guide or heuristic to frame our problem statements:

How can we [state the issue] . . . so that [state the conditions]?

Example:
How can we come to a decision about ownership of the wetlands . . . so that we address

- *Jobs of refinery workers.*
- *Revenue to the state.*
- *Ecology of the wetland.*
- *Clear cutting of the wetlands.*
- *Law protecting the wetlands.*
- *Political pressure.*
- *Political votes.*
- *Political jobs.*

Remember, this anticipated problem statement is a design tool for the teacher—not something we provide for the students. They must define the real problem for themselves. Students may go through several refinement cycles, but the struggle and experience of grasping the whole situation are essential. We want to engage our learners in the messiness of the situation so that they experience the tentativeness, incompleteness, and the desire to know more before they attempt to craft a solution.

Einstein once remarked that both the most difficult and the most critical part of problem solving is problem definition. The easiest way to begin would be to "give" students their problem, but if you did that, you would also take away the opportunity for students to develop important problem-sensing skills and inhibit their creativity, value building, and engagement. Defining the problem for students reinforces the notion that the task of problem solving is quick and easy: Follow the rules, march to conclusion, and justify it. Given the open-ended opportunity, students often identify issues and conditions that never occurred to the teacher.

Gather Information. As we plan PBL units, we usually gather an abundance of information from the community, the library, the Internet, and available experts. Remember that the students should only be given basic information on the problem and the larger questions to be resolved. This information may be in the form of a letter or a newspaper clipping. For one biomedical problem where students were in a role as consulting physicians, they received a phone message slip alerting them to a consultation appointment in two weeks (really their performance assessment), a radiologist's report, and the social worker's field notes on the patient. Once students identify what the root problem is and what they need to know, they will gather the necessary information from multiple sources. At this time, you may choose to satisfy some of their identified needs—or not.

Knowing What You'll Need to Do Once You've Arrived

We have now come full circle to a question posed earlier: What meaningful performance assessment will allow students to interact with the problem's real stakeholders and show their accumulated knowledge in an integrated and authentic way? Now that we are clear about the role or stakeholder position that students will take on as they immerse themselves in the problematic situation *and* we have anticipated the root problem they will identify, we can decide how they will bring their inquiry to a close. We want the final performance to provide an opportunity for authentic assessment of learners' thinking and actions in their role and circumstances, making a direct connection between the habits of mind nurtured in the classroom and those needed in the real world.

Over and over again, we have witnessed students rise to the occasion and outperform their teacher's grandest expectations. We have also seen the reverse—where student interest and enthusiasm for the problem inquiry flags as the inquiry winds down. What makes the difference between these two very different outcomes? *Learners want to know that their efforts will have consequences.* If they believe that someone will think about and value their work, they are more likely to undertake that work with enthusiasm and rigor.

Throughout the inquiry, students place themselves in the middle of the problem investigation. They interact authentically with the information, problem, and players. They own the problem and anticipate having some influence upon its resolution or at the very least a similar problem. Designing a performance assessment where students face real stakeholders or present information to them raises the stakes considerably. People who have actually lived the problem usually pose questions and challenges that probe for deeper levels of understanding and knowing, thus exposing the problem's rough edges. Staging the performance so that it mirrors how actual stakeholders might interact adds another measure of relevance. Figure 5.14 shows examples of performance scenarios based on specific roles.

It's Worth the Effort!

After a student group presented a proposed policy to a mock school board, one middle school student wrote this comment in a reflective journal entry:

> I'm a straight A student, but it's mostly because I know how to find answers in the textbooks. I've never had to defend my own answers—I think this is the first time I've ever had to think! COOL . . .

In an earlier journal entry, when students were still considering possible solutions, here is what one of this student's peers wrote:

It seems like when other teachers know our ideas are stupid, the ideas are dismissed. The teachers never say. the idea is stupid, but the way the ideas get dismissed lets us know we came up with a stupid idea. The way you [PBL teacher] . . . asked questions made us go all the way through our own thoughts. If it turned out the idea was stupid, it's because we figured it out ourselves.

FIGURE 5.14
Designing Authentic Performance Scenarios

Role or Perspective	Situation or Expectation	Performance Scenario
Environmental engineer	Advise city mayor.	Prepare proposal or white paper.
Citizen's focus group	Advise county agency.	Develop action plan.
Congressional staffer	Investigate viability of legislation.	Testify before a House subcommittee hearing.
Physician	Question a diagnosis.	Conduct a patient consultation.
City emergency worker	Prepare for unprecedented floods.	Design an emergency information pamphlet.
Student interest group	Challenge proposed action limiting access, rights, or privileges.	Make a presentation at a school board meeting.

Reprinted from Torp & Sage (1998), p. 62.

Here is what their PBL teacher wrote:

> There was no way I could have predicted that adolescents would be able to intellectualize the problem as clearly as they did. It was my contention that they wouldn't understand the larger problem present, didn't understand a school system's hierarchy, and shouldn't have input into decision making. However, the teens . . . happily disproved my predictions! . . . I guess I have to say those kids have jolted me back into the reality that just because they're kids doesn't mean they have to be babied!

Summary

The common threads woven through all the elements of design—context, students, and curriculum—enable us to design coherent PBL learning experiences. Healthy measures of openness and playfulness enable us to step outside familiar structures and see the relevant problems that reside in holistic real-world experiences.

Once you know the scope of your PBL adventure—where you're going, how you're going to get there, and what you'll need to know when you've arrived—you're ready to consider PBL implementation. Chapter 6 discusses new roles for teachers and students in PBL classrooms, then helps you consider this question: *Why, how, and what do I coach?*

6

How Do You Implement Problem-Based Learning?

ONCE YOU HAVE DESIGNED A PROBLEM YOU BELIEVE HAS worth and will engage your students, you are ready to begin implementing it. This chapter explores implementing PBL in your classroom.

Problem-based learning is one of a range of constructivist strategies for teaching and learning, based on philosophical positions we presented in earlier chapters. A helpful analogy for the work of teachers in PBL is the work of athletic coaches. Coaches typically work on the sidelines, supporting players in decision making and strategy selection. Because this analogy helps many people understand a teacher's role in PBL, we call teachers' work "coaching."

We have found that for most teachers beginning to explore PBL, becoming comfortable teaching within this role of coach is a profound learning experience. "How do I interact with my students? How do I manage this complex process? What kinds of things will my students and I be doing in PBL?" In this chapter, we also consider coaching in PBL.

New Roles for Teachers and Students

Again and again, PBL teachers with whom we have worked speak eloquently about the challenges inherent in rethinking their entire concept of teaching and learning (Sage & Torp, 1997). Students, too—particularly those who have been successful in a more traditional teaching setting—often struggle with their new role as active thinkers and learners and the higher degree of ambiguity they encounter in ill-structured problems. As Figure 6.1 shows, these roles evolve gradually. Students, over time, take an increased responsibility for learning as they develop a set of skills and habits of mind for becoming more self-directed. Teachers, over time, need to provide different kinds of supports for student learning, but teachers never become unnecessary; coaching is a highly active role. As teacher comments show, learning to guide involves trusting in the PBL experience and redefining control:

> I think I'm realizing more and more that fear was my major obstacle to begin with, and that the more I trust, the better I become as a PBL teacher. I was afraid that my students might not come through when the responsibility was in their hands for defining problem statements, for coming up with solution options, and what steps to take to pursue their solution options. I think that fear limited me in my coaching through my first year of trying PBL. This year I was able to pull back on that a little and hand the ball to them. The more I trust them, the more successful it is. I do much less limiting of students' options and thinking when I trust them in that way.
>
> —Mary Biddle, social studies teacher,
> Franklin Middle School, Champaign, IL

> It's the old control issue; you can't really control the journey, but you can help guide. We can decide what to do as facilitators—whether we need embedded instruction or something else.
>
> —Louise Robb, Principal,
> Fox Meadow Elementary School, South Elgin, IL,
> and former teacher, Barrington Middle School,
> Prairie Campus, Barrington, IL

> Being a guide was the hardest thing for us to learn to do—finding a balance between what students need to know now, so I need to teach a lesson about that, and letting them go explore and maybe get a little frustrated and come back and work with their information. The other thing we learned was to be in the role of a questioner instead of a teller, to ask good questions that lead them down the role of thinking: "How are you thinking about this? What evidence do you have for that? Have you thought of another point of view?" If we focused on the thinking questions, the content we wanted them to learn came out; they were able to find it.
>
> —Laurie Friedrich, staff development coordinator,
> West High School, Wauwatosa, WI

What Is Coaching?

> I think you make decisions about content. Is this something that is on the fringe that the students can be held responsible for because they missed it? Or is it a real central chord to where the problem is going? If so, then through coaching questions or some kind of dialogue I would ask enough for them to bring it up.
>
> —John Thompson, science/biology teacher,
> Illinois Mathematics and Science Academy, Aurora, IL

FIGURE 6.1
Evolving Roles in PBL

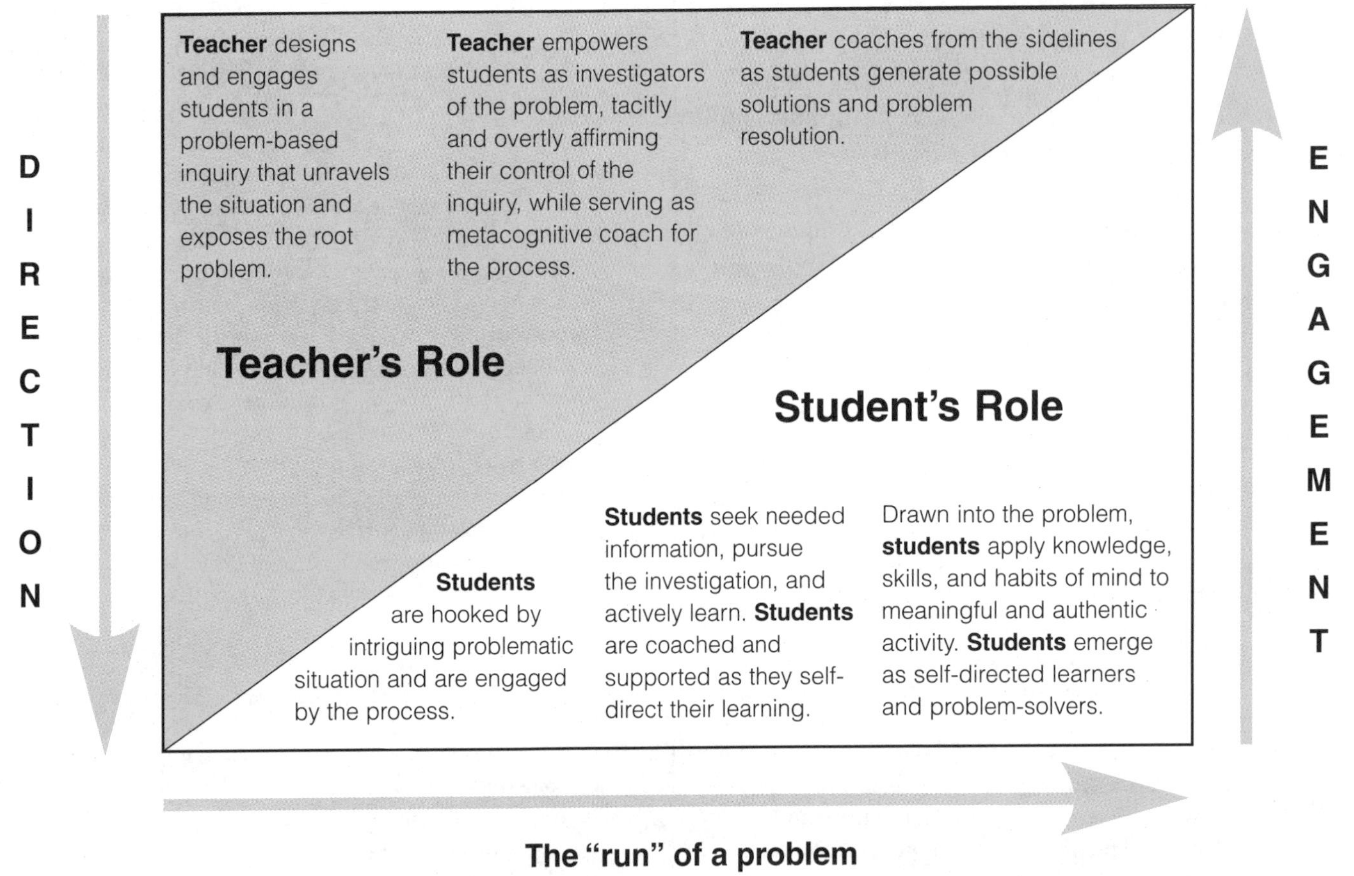

D
I
R
E
C
T
I
O
N

Teacher designs and engages students in a problem-based inquiry that unravels the situation and exposes the root problem.

Teacher empowers students as investigators of the problem, tacitly and overtly affirming their control of the inquiry, while serving as metacognitive coach for the process.

Teacher coaches from the sidelines as students generate possible solutions and problem resolution.

Teacher's Role

Student's Role

Students are hooked by intriguing problematic situation and are engaged by the process.

Students seek needed information, pursue the investigation, and actively learn. **Students** are coached and supported as they self-direct their learning.

Drawn into the problem, **students** apply knowledge, skills, and habits of mind to meaningful and authentic activity. **Students** emerge as self-directed learners and problem-solvers.

E
N
G
A
G
E
M
E
N
T

The "run" of a problem

Adapted from Torp & Sage (1998), p. 65. © 1996 Illinois Mathematics and Science Academy, Center for Problem-Based Learning, Aurora, IL.

The teacher in North American schools is faced with a mind-boggling array of mutually incompatible expectations and imperatives. . . . The practice of teaching is complex, uncertain, and dilemma-riddled.

—Clark (1988)

Both Thompson and Clark point out the complexity and constant stream of decision making inherent in any type of teaching, including coaching. As PBL teachers, we coach students' thinking, their communication—including the gathering and sharing of information—their group process, and their problem-solving strategies. Our role shifts from one of *control* of what and how students learn to one of *mediation* of student learning. This coaching role requires us to be as engaged in learning as our students and to develop a sense of flow in our teaching beliefs, actions, and decisions. Such work may initially cause some uneasiness, as Thompson's comments show:

I remember the first time I ran a problem—I kind of kept my fingers crossed under the desk the whole time, wondering if it was going to work. Now I've seen it work, and probably I'm more demanding in terms of the students, making them more responsible for their own research and learning.

In PBL, coaching is a process of goal setting, modeling, guiding, facilitating, monitoring, and providing feedback to students to support their active and self-directed thinking and learning. Teachers accomplish these goals by encouraging as much active learning as possible and by finding ways to make students' thinking visible.

Situation and Role

In this chapter, we use a particular problem experience to draw you into the process of coaching in PBL. John Thompson's ecology class used this PBL experience at IMSA:

Role and Situation: You are members of the Committee on the Environment and Natural Resources in the Minnesota House of Representatives. Wolf populations are increasing in Minnesota, and within a few years the species may no longer be protected under the federal Endangered Species Act. How would you explain your position on a newly proposed state wolf management plan to a group of your expert constituents? (In their role as state legislators, students received an actual piece of proposed legislation, Minnesota House Bill 1891, and had about 15 days to prepare for discussing it with a panel of experts.)

Teacher John Thompson provides an example of what he does for the wolf problem: "They've heard the term 'carrying capacity,' but they don't know that the carrying capacity has been calculated at 2,000 wolves. So once they figure that out, my next questions would be: 'Okay, now that we're 400 over, what does that mean, and how did the person you talked with figure out 2,000 was a capacity in the first place?' Well, that gets into some serious biology they wouldn't have gotten to if it had just been a point in some lecture. Now population dynamics have to be actively understood and applied to the situation."

To help accomplish these goals, Thompson assumes a supporting but still active sideline role (coach), offering help as needed and providing guidance as the students think, test strategies, and consider solutions. The big decision in each teaching/coaching moment, then, is deciding when to let the players play and when and how to intervene. As a former student recalls, John Thompson decided to "let her play":

> We had a hearing where we brought in some people, and we had to stand up and defend the position we'd taken. I was speaking for a group who'd been working on one portion of the research. At the end, this man said, "Have you considered how your wolf plan will affect the Native American populations in the region? They fall under different laws because of their religious practices and beliefs."
>
> And I said, "I didn't have a clue!" We completely missed this aspect, because we were focusing somewhere else. That taught me to be a lot more thorough in research we're doing and to get different perspectives.

In the next example, Thompson describes how he intervened using a deliberate instructional event to make sure students encountered important ecology content in this problem:

> Hunting is the weak issue now; it's just coming slower than I would have thought. Now it's time to bring it in. Fortunately, I've done the preparation and gotten all the props so we can do something that will look realistic and infuse a little drama into the problem. So what the students are going to get is a phone call from a hunter who asks them to go out and look at this kill site on Tuesday. When they look at the kill site, the

object is to understand that this species is severely weakened by arthritis, and that wolves kill the most vulnerable among them, but that hunting doesn't focus on the same segment of the population.

The following is an excerpt from a conversation between Thompson and one of his students, Chris. The exchange occurred just after Chris and two classmates, trying to locate more information about what Minnesota counties would be affected by House Bill 1891, finished talking with an expert from the International Wolf Center in Ely, Minnesota.

> *Chris:* She's never heard of the bill. . . . It sounded like the only way we're really going to find out the actual information we need is by talking to the author of the bill.
>
> *Mr. Thompson:* Well, let's go back. Be more specific; tell me exactly what you're trying to find out, plus what you've already learned from this phone conversation (facilitating student understanding through *diagnosing and questioning*).
>
> *Chris:* We're looking for the counties that are going to have wolves introduced.
>
> *Mr. Thompson:* Okay. Did you ask her where wolves are currently found (*questioning*)? You said something about the carrying capacity is exceeded.
>
> *Chris:* Yeah, that's what she said.
>
> *Mr. Thompson:* Did you get a number on the carrying capacity (*questioning*)?
>
> *Chris:* No.
>
> *Mr. Thompson:* Okay. So what you have are bits and pieces of information. The question is, how do you

begin to connect these? I would collectively (*modeling*)—the three of you—say: "What did I find out in this phone call? What do I know from the bill?" (*questioning*) and "What's my next 'need to know'?" So when we go back upstairs (*managing group work*), you can say, "Look, I've just found out this and this, but it brings up a new set of questions like, I don't know what the carrying capacity is. . . ."

    Chris: She was very curious about the bill.

    Mr. Thompson: I'd imagine so. But look at the point. You're now talking to a real person who is curious about what you're doing. All of a sudden you're informing the real people instead of the real people informing you. That puts you in a pretty knowledgeable position (*using role and drama*). . . . So while we can feel good about ourselves on that one, let's look at what the next level of questions is. She told us this. What are the implications (*mentoring*)?

As this coaching episode helps illustrate, and as we have learned from our experiences and observing others, *how* and *what* we coach breaks down into two broad processes:

- Exposing and facilitating student thinking and moving to deeper levels of understanding—through *diagnosing, mentoring, questioning,* and *modeling.*
- Managing the PBL process itself in your classroom—*adapting the PBL process, using role and drama, managing group work,* and *monitoring student engagement.*

Ongoing coaching makes these two processes possible, as well as the instruction and assessments *embedded* in the PBL process (see Figure 6.2).

Facilitating Student Understanding

Teachers of problem-based learning must coach students' thinking, inquiry, and metacognition as students work to solve problems. This process has several parts: diagnosing, mentoring, questioning, and modeling.

Diagnosing

    One important role coaches must play in facilitating student understanding is educational diagnosis (Barrows, 1988). The coach must identify students' learning needs and their level of engagement, so that students don't slide through a PBL experience without ever understanding the problem and its solution. Coaches observe students, listen to what they are saying (and not saying), carefully look at assessments embedded in the PBL experience, and *ask questions.*

    Another format for diagnosis is asking students to map or web their current understanding of the problem, as teacher John Thompson did early in the PBL experience. Individual students may be struggling with reasoning, locating appropriate information, understanding concepts discussed by the group, or understanding the nature of the problem itself. Coaches can intervene with personal assistance or through encouraging the student's group to provide assistance. We suggest using focused, metacognitive questions, such as, "Were you able to find all the resources you wanted?" or "Does the way you have put that together make sense to you?" to challenge students in particular areas of difficulty.

    We want to make very clear that we don't believe *teaching* is a dirty word (Harris & Graham, 1996) in our model

FIGURE 6.2
Using PBL Coaching to Help Construct Meaning

Teachers as Active Coaches

Facilitating Understanding

- Diagnosing needs
- Mentoring learning
- Encouraging process
- Questioning thinking
- Modeling inquiry

Managing the Process

- Adapting the PBL process
- Using role-play and drama
- Managing work groups
- Monitoring engagement
- Assessing in process

Problem as Organizing Center

- Focusing inquiry
- Embedding instruction
- Assessing learning

Students as Active Learners

Thinking

- Questioning
- Investigating
- Adapting
- Projecting
- Evaluating
- Constructing meaning

of PBL coaching. Successful PBL coaches diagnose students' learning needs and then arrange whatever support students require. Direct instruction may be appropriately embedded when students need to know some background or facts or to learn a particular skill. For example, the day students made the phone call outlined in the conversation between Chris and Thompson, Thompson discovered that a number of his students didn't understand how to use long-distance information services. He led a brief, focused discussion on how to do that before students dispersed to place their various calls.

Mentoring

Another important part of facilitating student understanding is the coach's role as mentor to students (Duffy & Savery, 1995). PBL coaches (mentors) seek out and value their students' (protégés') points of view. The coach does not take over thinking for students by telling them what to do or how to think, but does challenge them by inquiring at the leading edge of their thinking. The mentor and the protégés are learners together; the mentor helps students build bridges from their present understanding to new, more complex understandings (Brooks, J. G., & Brooks, 1999). The coach as mentor must also maintain appropriate levels of challenge during the PBL experience, prompting students to move further in their thinking but not pushing so hard that students become frustrated and give up.

One way Thompson and other coaches mentor students is to assign entries in student thinking logs. He may ask a focused question like, "What is your current understanding of predators?" and read and respond to student responses. Such logs are useful not only as measures of student thinking and possible frustration levels, but also as assessments embedded throughout a PBL experience.

Questioning

To facilitate student understanding, coaches must hold students to strict benchmarks of good thinking and reasoning, including specificity, defensibility, examination of bias, and consideration of opposing views. Probably the best way teachers can do this work is by questioning. Well-placed questions that probe students to think further or challenge them to reconsider their thinking not only help students consider different aspects of a problem situation, but also encourage them to become critical thinkers. Questions may also serve to redirect students or prompt them to set goals for their own inquiry.

We find that Karen Kitchener's (1983) three-level model of cognitive processing, shown in Figure 6.3, is a helpful structure for considering questioning in an ill-structured problem experience:

- Cognition
- Metacognition
- Epistemic cognition

At the *cognitive* level, students compute, read, perceive, and comprehend information. *Metacognitive* questions help students monitor their own thinking process and consider

FIGURE 6.3
Three Levels of Thinking and Questioning

Level 1: Cognition (Thinking)	Level 2: Metacognition (Learning about thinking)	Level 3: Epistemic Cognition (Nature of knowing in ill-structured problems)
Questions coaches might ask: What have you learned? Are you sure? What seems important here? What does this mean for our problem? Do you have enough facts to suggest _____?	*Questions coaches might ask:* What, if anything, about your goals and strategies needs to change? What kinds of resources have been most helpful to you so far? Have you considered _____? (process or strategy)	*Questions coaches might ask:* How do you know? What can we know? To what degree of certainty? What is at stake? What solution fits best with the criteria in our problem statement?

Reprinted from Torp & Sage (1998), p. 71. *Source:* Adapted from Kitchener (1983).

appropriate strategies. *Epistemic cognition* refers to individuals' understanding of the nature of problems and includes knowledge about the limits and certainty of knowing, and the criteria for knowing. Figure 6.4 gives general guidelines for questioning as PBL coaches.

Modeling

A fourth way coaches facilitate student understanding is by modeling the kinds of thinking behaviors they want

FIGURE 6.4
Guidelines for Questioning as PBL Coaches

Actively listen to what students are *and* are not saying.

Ask questions that require a rich response.

Use all three levels of cognitive questioning.

Avoid yes-or-no questions and one-word answers.

Pause to allow thoughtful responses.

Encourage and allow the conversation to reside among students as much as possible.

Avoid the temptation to correct immediately or interrupt.

Encourage support and justification of ideas—probe to extend student thinking.

Challenge data, assumptions, and sources.

Avoid feedback that cues students to the "rightness" of their statements; probe students frequently so probing is not viewed only as a cue for "wrongness."

Reprinted from Torp & Sage (1998), p. 72.

their students to exhibit. Coaches may model openness to complexity and ambiguity, and willingness to engage in ambiguous situations. They may also model patience, particularly when listening to others and being open to what others are saying. As coaches, we should talk about and model our thinking and problem solving, not dispense information. We can also model metacognition through examples of our own thinking strengths and weaknesses, and what we have learned from solving problems. Perhaps most important is to model respecting the ideas and opinions of others through acknowledging the students' perspectives, as the coach models a willingness and ability to be a learner along with students.

Managing the PBL Process

A second major emphasis for coaches is managing the implementation of PBL in their particular classrooms. This management includes adapting the PBL process, using role and drama, managing group work, and monitoring student engagement.

Adapting the PBL Process

The template of teaching and learning events we presented in Chapter 4 is a suggested structure for implementing PBL, not a rigid prescription. We highlight essential elements of PBL in Chapter 2, with the most important parameter being centering learning around an ill-structured problem. Beyond those parameters, the template of events can be flexible for use with many different students. We might apply what David Perkins (1999) calls "pragmatic constructivism"—if one particular approach does not help students learn, try another. Some coaches, for example, choose to have students develop a problem statement *before* the students identify what they know and need to know. These coaches believe defining the nature of the problem first helps keep the "knows" and "need to knows" more focused.

Many coaches work with the whole class on the "know/ need-to-know" and "problem statement" events. Others, like teacher John Thompson during the wolf problem, choose to have students work in small groups to develop their own "know" and "need-to-know" lists before the class comes together as a whole. One reason for Thompson's decision was the presence of a high number of introverted students in the ecology class who felt more comfortable sharing in small groups than in the whole class setting. He also chose to wait until several days into the problem experience before developing problem statements, because he felt the problem statements would be too vague to be helpful until the students had gathered some information about the proposed bill. Students then individually mapped their understanding of the problem. Figures 6.5 and 6.6 show maps that represent students' growing understanding and knowledge base about the problem.

Using Role and Drama

Frequently in a problem, coaches engage students by having them take on a role that might be unfamiliar to them

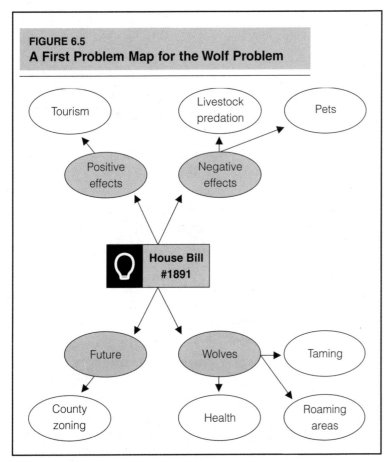

FIGURE 6.5
A First Problem Map for the Wolf Problem

Adapted from Torp & Sage (1998), p. 73.

that intimately involves them in the problem as insiders, so students own the problem and have an investment in solving it. Coaches are instrumental in preparing students for their roles by discussing role-play and often by providing props and scenery that help students manage their roles.

In the wolf problem, where students took on the role of state legislators, Thompson prepared students the day before they met the problem by describing the "suspension of disbelief" as similar to the mind-set we develop when watching a movie or seeing a play. The next day, when students entered the class, the teacher gave a signal indicating the beginning of their problem experience, and they understood they were now in the role of state legislators. Throughout the problem experience, he also used props, such as realistic briefing packets that included the state seal and name placards for each representative.

Managing Group Work

Another important part of the PBL process for coaches is managing student group work. Group work can help promote creative problem solving and higher-order thinking skills as well as develop an appreciation of diversity and teamwork (Cohen, 1994). Cooperative group work has also been linked with higher performance on complex, ill-structured problems (Qin, Johnson, & Johnson, 1995). Some students enter PBL with a good deal of group work experiences (positive or negative); other students have no such experience. Yet because the typical expectation in PBL is that students will work in groups both for information gathering and sharing and for

(refer to Chapter 5 for more detail on role playing). The key to role-play is to learn to suspend disbelief to "get into the role" (Center for Problem-Based Learning, 1996b). As the coach, you will help move students to a level of role playing

FIGURE 6.6
A Later Problem Map for the Wolf Problem

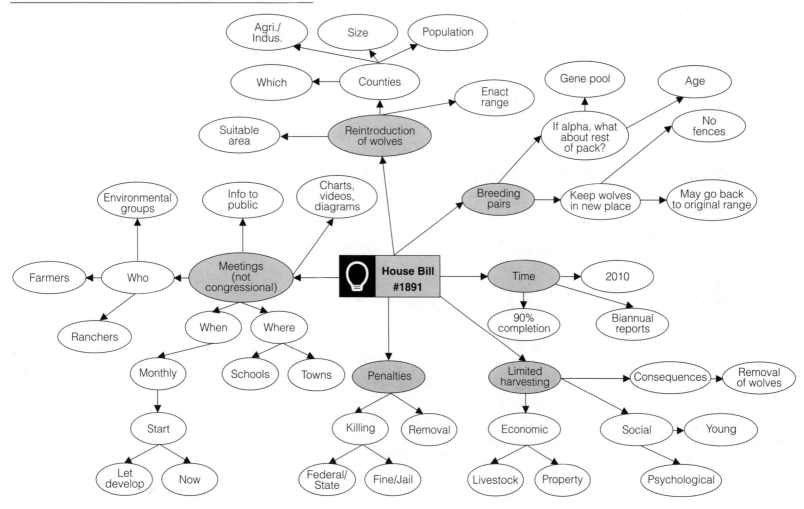

Reprinted from Torp & Sage (1998), p. 74.

presenting their solutions, effective preparation for, and management of, group work are essential. PBL coaches, particularly with students inexperienced in group work, may need to prepare students in areas such as

- Listening.
- Reflecting on what has been said.
- Allowing everyone to contribute.
- Sharing information with all members of the group.
- Pulling ideas together.
- Finding out if the group is ready to make a decision.
- Ensuring individual and group accountability.

Elizabeth Cohen's book *Designing Groupwork* (1994) and Spencer Kagan's book *Cooperative Learning* (1994) have excellent suggestions for activities that PBL coaches might use to prepare students for group work or to assist with group problems that arise during a PBL experience.

Two particular areas of challenge in group work are (for the students) in the sharing of information and (for the coaches) in assessing performance. One strategy PBL coaches often use for information gathering is for a small group of students to work on particular "need-to-know" questions the class has identified. How can the information that the group gathers best be shared with the entire class? The jigsaw method works well: Experts on particular questions are divided among groups so that each group has one expert for presenting solutions in each important area. Other coaches, particularly those with younger students, may choose to have expert groups present information through visual or oral class presentations. Coaches must also manage information gathering and sharing sessions so that they last as long as necessary for the complexity and nature of the problem, but not so long that students become bored or have to endure repetitive information.

Assessments for group work must include both individual and group accountability. Some coaches accomplish this goal by structuring individual assessments such as review of journals or logs while students are working on the problem and planning the presentation of solutions as group accountability. Coaches often develop rubrics with their students for scoring culminating performances, such as oral presentations, displays, and videos. Rubrics help members of the presentation groups not only take more ownership in the overall quality of the presentation, but also be aware of which indicators of quality will form the assessment.

Monitoring Student Engagement

Finally, throughout the PBL process, coaches must monitor the engagement of students and intervene with nonparticipating students when necessary. Thompson identified several students who often physically isolated themselves from the rest of the class and who were not contributing substantively to information gathering. A large part of his class time in PBL was whole-class discussion, during which time small groups shared the information they had gathered. He instituted the use of "talking chips" (Kagan, 1994): Students had to contribute to the discussion enough times to use up their chips, but could not contribute when their chips were gone. This strategy also works well with students who tend to dominate group discussions. Coaches may also, through probing questions, need to identify why particular students have chosen to disengage themselves from the problem, and perhaps encourage them to pursue an area of inquiry that is personally motivating.

Embedding Instruction and Assessment

> The primary purpose of classroom assessment
> is to inform teaching and improve learning. This
> premise suggests assessment be viewed as an ongoing
> process instead of a single event at the conclusion of
> instruction. . . . Assessment for learning recognizes
> the mutually supportive relationship between instruc-
> tion and assessment. Like a Möbius strip where one
> side appears to seamlessly blend into the other, class-
> room assessment should reflect and promote good
> instruction.
>
> —McTighe (1996)

The glue that holds together all the coaching strategies presented in this chapter is an understanding of the relationship among curriculum, instruction, and assessment. Ongoing assessments throughout the problem experience help coaches determine students' learning needs and then embed instruction in various authentic ways.

Embedded instruction refers to events planned by the PBL teacher to help students explore important information related to the problem. Coaches can schedule these events to occur during the design of the problem or during the course of the problem, as students identify a need for knowing certain information. For example, the best information about a problem often resides with people. Teachers may plan to invite local experts on a particular issue as guest speakers or mentors for students. Typically, this type of instructional event looks like a question-and-answer session, in which students may ask their own "need-to-know" questions rather than listen to an expert's presentation.

Sometimes teachers we encounter initially think that incorporating lessons on particular content or skills is not allowed in PBL or other constructivist strategies. On the contrary! The problematic situation often provides a perfect context for students to have a need for knowing certain information. Lessons then embed the learning in an authentic context. For example, Thompson had identified hunting as a critical predator issue in designing the wolf problem. When students in the late stages of information gathering had not yet emphasized this crucial aspect of the proposed legislation, he inserted an authentic lesson on hunting (the kill site demonstration mentioned earlier in the chapter). He embedded this lesson authentically in the problem by asking a colleague to role-play an irate hunter who contacted several students by telephone to ask them to examine the kill site on their school property. Thompson also embedded instructional events by planning field trips to observe wolves at a local zoo and a regional wolf park. Coaches may plan to work with small groups on such needed skills as letter writing or mathematical computation as students encounter a need to know such knowledge for locating information or solving the problem.

Assessment Possibilities in PBL

PBL Event	Products	Forms	Criteria
Problem Clarification and Identification *Teacher Role:* Read and listen to students present individual problem statements.	Problem statement	Journal entry Problem map Oral presentation Poster Abstract Statement displays	Considers: Nature of problem Problem complexity Operativeness Solvability
Plan Development *Teacher Role:* Review tasks and listen to students clarify plans.	Plan	Task analysis Time line Gantt chart Flow chart Steps Proposal Budget	Uses tasks that control extraneous variables and are Comprehensive Logical Clear Related to nature of problem
Data Collection and Inference Testing *Teacher Role:* Observe, review notes and data, and read journals.	Data records Use of tools Practice of skills	Tables Charts Field notes Microscope use Instrumentation Interviews Observations Quizzes using notes	Records data accurately. Uses tools correctly. Practices skills precisely.
Data Analysis *Teacher Role:* Read and analyze tables, graphs, distribution, etc.	Summary of findings Frequency tables and statistical tables	Summary statements with supporting data Compiled evidence	Uses correct statistical techniques. Makes logical interpretations. Shares collaboratively.
Synthesizing Capstone Performance *Teacher Role:* Observe and assess performance.	Exhibition and recital	News article Poem Decision Recommendation Argument Speech Debate	Displays inventiveness. Relates solution or decision to problem definition. Incorporates problem parameters in solution.

Reprinted from Torp & Sage (1998), p. 77. *Source:* Adapted from Musial (1996).

Embedded assessments provide teachers with a sense of students' thinking at various points in a problem sequence. They also prompt students to address relationships among important events and to learn during the problem experience. Such ongoing assessments may take a variety of forms to fit the learner and the problem experience (see Figure 6.7). Based on assessment results, coaches may redirect the problem through instructional events or work with particular students to aid their understanding of the whole and parts of the problem.

Thompson used two forms of embedded assessment in the wolf problem: problem maps (see Figures 6.5 and 6.6) and thinking logs. He could look at each map and determine student learning needs at that time. He could choose to have students map their understanding of the problem several times, and use the evolving maps and comparisons with an expert map as forms of assessment. Thompson also read and responded to student log entries periodically throughout the problem to assess their progress and diagnose their learning needs. (See Figure 6.7 for different methods of assessing performance in a PBL unit.)

Summary

In this chapter on implementing PBL, we discussed the teacher's role as coach and the students' role as active learners. We discussed why, how, and what we coach. Finally, we discussed in depth the PBL coach's main responsibilities, including facilitating student understanding, managing the PBL process, and embedding instruction and assessment throughout the sequence of the problem.

7

How Do You Assess Learning in and Through Problem-Based Learning?

WHEN PLANNING A PBL EXPERIENCE, OF COURSE YOU KEEP your learners in mind. Your goals are clear. You've targeted learning standards, mapped out instructional strategies, and arranged for plentiful resources, but what about assessment? At the Illinois ASCD Conference in 1993, Roger Farr spoke with conviction about assessment, capturing in one sentence its essence, "How do you know a good one when you see one?" In this chapter, we look briefly at the general topic of assessment; then we examine assessment through the lens of PBL.

Focusing Our Assessment Vision

Several years ago, Steven Covey (1990) made the phrase, "Begin with the end in mind!" well known as one of the seven habits in his book, *The Seven Habits of Highly Effective People*. This guiding principle is known in many

How Do You Assess Learning in and Through Problem-Based Learning?

85

professions as *backwards planning*. Before entering the teaching profession, one of the authors learned quickly as a production scheduler for a major television manufacturer that arriving at where you need to be demands that you know where you are going. That concept holds especially true when designing curriculum, whether it's problem-based or not.

Principles of Instruction

In *Basic Principles of Curriculum and Instruction* (1949), Ralph Tyler set forth four questions about curriculum planning and assessment that remain valid today. To his four basic questions we have added a number of follow-ups that apply directly to the discussion of PBL.

1. What educational purposes should the school seek to attain?
- Are national standards useful in deciding what students need to know, apply, and value?
- Which state learning standards apply?
- Has your local school district defined goals and standards?
- What are your goals for your students?

2. How can teachers select learning experiences that are likely to be useful in attaining these objectives?
- What is developmentally appropriate for your students?
- Have you considered the interests of your students?
- Who needs to have input into the selection process?

3. How can you organize learning experiences for effective instruction?
- Direct instruction?
- Discovery learning?
- Concept attainment?
- Problem-based learning?
- In other words, what instructional strategy fits the purposes and the specific learning experiences?

4. How can you calculate the effectiveness of learning experiences?
- How do you know that what you intended actually happened?
- You wanted them to learn something—did they?
- How well did they learn it? What evidence do you have?
- Was this learning experience worth repeating?
- Does it need to be modified? How?

Ralph Tyler had a great deal of respect for teachers and the important work that they do, as do we. Tyler spoke of teachers' assessment practices and the need to use common sense, but he noted with remorse that "the only problem with common sense is that it's so uncommon" (Riddings-Nowakowski, 1981).

Tyler believed that learning takes place through the student's active behaviors. In other words, a student learns by doing, not by watching and listening to what the teacher does. As educators, we need clarity about what we want students to know and do—and, as Roger Farr said, to know it when we see it.

Bloom's Taxonomy

Over the years, many people have contributed to our ability to know learning when we see it. One such researcher was Benjamin Bloom. He and his colleagues (Bloom & Krathwohl, 1956) developed a classification system (or taxonomy) for three overlapping domains of intellectual behavior important in learning (cognitive, affective, and psychomotor).

We are concerned most often in the classroom with the six areas of the *cognitive domain*. Particular behaviors characterize this domain, and certain verbs signal the activities that accompany them.

Knowledge	arrange	list	recognize
	define	memorize	relate
	duplicate	name	recall
	label	order	repeat

Compre-hension	classify	identify	restate
	describe	indicate	review
	discuss	locate	select
	explain	relate	translate
	express	report	

Application	apply	illustrate	sketch
	choose	interpret	solve
	demonstrate	operate	use
	dramatize	practice	write
	employ	schedule	

Analysis	analyze	contrast	examine
	appraise	criticize	experiment
	calculate	differentiate	question
	categorize	discriminate	test
	compare	distinguish	

Synthesis	arrange	design	prepare
	assemble	develop	propose
	collect	formulate	set up
	compose	manage	write
	construct	organize	
	create	plan	

Evaluation	appraise	defend	score
	argue	estimate	select
	assess	evaluate	support
	attach	judge	value
	choose	predict	
	compare	rate	

The *affective domain* relates to emotions, attitudes, appreciations, and values, like enjoying, respecting, and supporting. This domain includes behaviors indicating attitudes of interest, concern, and responsibility; an ability to listen and respond to others; and an ability to demonstrate attitudes that fit the situation and the field of study.

Psychomotor learning is displayed through physical skills like coordination, manipulation, grace, strength, and speed—activities that use fine motor or gross motor skills. Verbs related to this domain include bend, grasp, handle, operate, reach, relax, shorten, stretch, write, and perform.

Facets of Understanding

Today, Grant Wiggins and Jay McTighe continue to sharpen our focus relating to assessment so that we see valued learning outcomes more clearly. They propose six facets of understanding (1998) that provide further insight into students' comprehension.

- *Explanation*—articulating not just the what, but also the why and the how of a thing
- *Interpretation*—bringing an explanation into the realm of personal experience
- *Application*—taking knowledge and skill from the learning experience and using it in a different circumstance (time, distance, discipline, context, etc.)
- *Perspective*—looking into a thing and emerging with one's own insights and point of view

- *Empathy*—getting inside another person's feelings and worldview
- *Self-knowledge*—knowing what you know and what you don't know and how your own frame of reference (culture, ignorance, style, etc.) distorts or frames your perception

Wiggins and McTighe propose that these facets are not a theory of how we understand, but rather of how educators recognize student understanding or misunderstanding when they see it. What can we see or hear or experience through a student's product or performance (paper, story, presentation, drama, model, experiment, etc.) that signals understanding? The clarity of each instance of assessment and its contribution to the whole picture—much like the facets of a gem—add to our insight into the student's understanding. Taken together they tell us much more than any one facet alone. Figure 7.1 presents a matrix of some questions teachers can ask to assess these facets in the context of problem-based learning. For example, what is the effect of *empathy* on the way a student tries to solve a problem?

Assessment Through the Lens of PBL

As we have worked to clarify assessment in problem-based learning, we have come to see varying possibilities and perspectives.

FIGURE 7.1
Understanding by Design and PBL

Facet of Understanding	Explanation	Interpretation	Application
Perspective	Does a stakeholder's perspective influence the relevant details of an explanation?	Does a stakeholder's perspective skew his or her interpretation of the facts of a situation?	Do the skills and knowledge that a stakeholder brings to a situation have an effect on the potential solution or resolution?
Empathy	If students truly recognize the collective ownership of a problem, are they able to sense the feelings/values of other stakeholders?	Do students take into account the positions of others when generating possible solutions?	In devising potential solutions, do students consider and incorporate the synergy of varied skill and knowledge bases?
Self-Knowledge	Do students recognize multiple layers to an explanation? Or do they recognize that they lack sufficient knowledge and thus need to investigate?	Are students able to set aside who they are enough to be able to step into another's worldview?	Do students apply relevant knowledge and skills to the effective resolution of the problem? Can they call on information that was learned through the problem, in this course, in other courses, or in life?

From the Perspective of Learning Coaches

As learning coaches, we need to find out what students are actually learning in the midst of the problem-based experience.

- What are students grasping? Do I need to provide embedded instruction to support learning?

- What do they still need to know to be able to identify the central problem? Do they need other resources? What questions do I pose to prompt their thinking in that direction?
- Are some students charging ahead or lagging behind? How can I provide for their needs through support or additional challenge?

Coaches/teachers also need information about other aspects of the students' learning life, as follows:

- Identify specific knowledge or skills that students are lacking, but recognize that instruction is not appropriate at this time. Students may also have a firm grasp of the complexities of a tangential issue/concept that you were planning to teach next month.

From the Perspective of Assessors and Evaluators

As assessors, we also need information for our roles in communicating grades and scores for accountability purposes:

- How do we, as professionals, manage our conflicting roles? How do we put aside the intimate, personal role of teacher and coach to become the objective, impersonal assessor and communicator of data who assigns a grade—excellent or poor, *A* or *F*, 50 percent or 100 percent, satisfactory or unsatisfactory?
- How do we communicate information about a student's achievement to parents?
- How does the system communicate information about students' achievement to the community?

As evaluators of programs, we need information about activities, units, or programs that will ensure continuous improvement of our educational system and our own personal practice.

- Does this program enable students to become self-directed learners?
- Are students aware of their own personal learning styles, and do they use such knowledge to map effective strategies for learning, study, and project completion?
- Does the program demonstrate collective knowledge and skill mastery while maintaining student interest in and enthusiasm for learning?

From our experience, we have identified five essential questions to consider when planning assessments:

- Why must we assess learning?
- What do you need to know to conduct an assessment?
- What forms—product or performance—might that assessment take? (quiz, paper, memo, chart, poster, video, tall tale, service project, small group collaborative work plan, etc.)
- How will the assessment take place? (proctored setting, classroom, take-home, one-on-one assessment interview, juried performance, portfolio review panel, etc.)
- The concluding and overarching question encompasses two concerns: *Who will receive the information—and how will they use it?* Depending on the answers, we know what stakes—and stakeholders—are involved.

From the Perspective of the Context

Assessing student learning in PBL is always done in the context of the problematic situation. Such assessment is designed for teachers to monitor the thinking and dispositions of the student and to subsequently adjust the learning experience, or as J. G. Brooks and Brooks (1999) put it, "Assessment and teaching [are] merged in service to the learner" (p. 91). We could also think of such assessment as developing a "model" of the student (von Glasersfeld, 1993) in which teachers gain an understanding of the conceptual structures in the students' heads so they may better teach students to learn. Finally, assessment serves the important purpose of evaluating student attainment of significant outcomes identified for the PBL experience.

We see two clear purposes for assessment: assessment *for* learning and assessment *of* learning.

Assessment *for* Learning. By assessment *for* learning, we mean assessment that helps to serve the learning process in some way—by providing information meaningful for either the teacher or the learner during the learning process. Most often, this is nongraded assessment in the form of *feedback, adjustment, refocusing,* and *coaching.* Remember that mistakes are part of the learning process. Learners who are penalized for making errors *or* rewarded for making on-target responses often shut down and become overly cautious and do not fully participate at all levels—intellectually and emotionally.

When teachers assess *for* learning, *risk taking is maximized,* though this is still a fragile type of behavior in classrooms today. But teacher/coaches can provide substantial safety nets for students who take risks: Through even-handed responses (written, audible, or facial); through coaching and mentoring; and through data-collection practices that signal opportunities for continued learning, teachers can use assessment that enhances the learning process.

Assessment *of* Learning. By assessment *of* learning, we mean assessment that aids documentation and decision-making in some way:

- By providing information relative to *expectations* (goals, standards, benchmarks, stated performance, or proficiency levels).
- By providing information relative to the *comparison or placement* of students (overall class performance, performance relative to another group—whether local, state, or national) within a group or against another individual or group.

Mistakes are expected and help to differentiate one student's performance from another student's performance, one class's performance from another class's performance, or one school's performance from another school's performance—and so on.

When teacher/coaches reflect high levels of concern or anxiety about potential results, *risk-taking is minimized and replaced by high levels of caution.* Students pick up on this anxiety and match it. Teachers and students recognize the stakes involved. Results are fixed and are used to determine a terminal outcome, one that signals an end to this learning experience. This end-point could be the end of a project, a unit of study, a semester, a course, an academic year, a transition point from elementary to middle school, from middle school to high school, from high school to college, or a terminal degree—bachelors, masters, doctorate, and so forth.

The matrix in Figure 7.2 helps to clarify the what, why, and when of assessment in and through PBL both *for* and *of* learning.

A PBL Learning Experience: Bubonic Plague Example

To illustrate the assessment possibilities in and through PBL, we highlight a problem that Bernie Hollister, a master social science teacher, designed, developed, and refined to engage students in thinking about the plague in the United States and the variables that contribute to its spread or containment. According to Hollister:

> Plague cases have occurred every year in the United States since the 1970s, and no one seems to have a

FIGURE 7.2
Assessment in and Through PBL

PBL Assessment	Assessment *for* Learning	Assessment *of* Learning
Assessment in PBL	This type of formative assessment informs ongoing learning, coaching, and embedded instruction (planned and/or situational) during the run of the PBL experience. Students rely on this information to adjust their learning and performance expectations.	This type of summative assessment provides information about knowledge and skill proficiency during the run of the PBL experience. Students are aware that they "will be graded" on these assessments that target specific knowledge sets, skills, or strategies.
Assessment Through PBL	This type of formative assessment informs ongoing instructional needs in the course or class that go beyond the scope of the PBL experience. Students are usually unaware of this information as it triggers actions by the teacher to set up situational groups or to modify course plans to better meet learning needs.	This type of summative assessment provides information about knowledge and skill integration, application, and competencies evident through PBL experiences, and more traditional pedagogies and assessment practices. Students are aware of this type of information as it relates to the authentic assessment of research paper, projects, problem investigations, and presentations where analytic or descriptive rubrics provide an overall assessment and a grade.

convincing and definitive reason why they occur in relatively few states: California, Colorado, Arizona, and New Mexico having the majority of the cases. Of course, this lack of a "right" answer connects beautifully with PBL, and that is why we construct a problem around plague.

Students take on the role of epidemiologists to examine CDC (Centers for Disease Control) data from outbreaks of bubonic plague in the United States during 1988 (http://www.imsa.edu/~bernie/plaguedata1988.html) and 1993 (http://www.imsa.edu/~bernie/plaguedata1993.html). In the following sections, we look at each stage of the PBL assignment and discuss what aspects of assessment apply to each.

Meet the Problem

Students as CDC epidemiologists are charged with investigating plague cases reported in 1988 and 1993. They engage in either small or large group discussion about what is known from limited information.

Assessment *for* Learning. Coaches systematically question students according to Bloom's lower levels (knowledge, comprehension, application): Where are most of the plague cases found? When do they occur?

During this aspect of PBL we firmly believe that all assessment serves teaching and learning and, as such, is diagnostic. Nothing is graded at this stage.

Know/Need to Know

Students as epidemiologists chart what they know, think, and need to know to better understand the situation. Groups or individuals take on aspects of the investigation to bring new knowledge to the team.

Assessment *for* Learning. Systematic questioning continues at higher levels (analysis, synthesis, evaluation) interspersed with metacognitive and epistemic questioning (see Figures 7.3 and 7.4):

- What is bubonic plague? Is it caused by a bacterium? By a virus? Is it something else?
- What are the animal vectors that help it spread? How does it spread—or does it—from one human to another?

During this aspect of PBL we firmly believe that, again, all assessment serves teaching and learning and, as such, is diagnostic. Nothing is graded at this stage, either.

Gather and Share Information

Students gather relevant information from multiple sources and glean pertinent facts to share with the group through charting, jigsaw, abstracts, discussion groups, and so forth.

Assessment *for* Learning. Questioning continues using probing and challenging information. Assumptions increase. Coaches need to ensure that students are focused on the science of plague and to coach learning in that direction.

- How is plague diagnosed? How is it cured? Does a vaccine exist? What are the morbidity and mortality rates?
- Is the microorganism that causes contemporary plague the same as Black Death? How might we determine this?
- How can one make intelligent inferences from the data? What are those inferences?

Assessment *of* Learning. As students build a knowledge base, expectations for conceptual understanding are high.

- Interim responses to supervisor's questions are presented in the form of telephone messages or some other form of intermediate communication.
- Presentations, memos, charts, and matrices of the findings of subgroups are shared with the entire class. With a larger problem, students will form targeted investigative groups, yet all need to know and understand critical information uncovered by each of the groups.
- Concept or mind mapping of the known information takes place, and the relationships become evident or begin building.

Defining the Problem Statement

With the situation, their background knowledge, and other information gathered and shared, students formulate a tentative problem statement to focus the inquiry.

FIGURE 7.3
Levels of Questioning in PBL

Cognitive-Level Questions:

- ? Are you sure?
- ? How reliable is ______? How valid is ______?
- ? Have you considered ______?
- ? Tell me more.
- ? What if ______?
- ? What do you mean?
- ? What is going on here?
- ? Where does this fit?
- ? Who needs to be considered?
- ? Do we have enough facts to suggest ______?
- ? How reasonable is ______?
- ? Can everyone define ______?
- ? If what Ann and Liz say is true, do you still believe ________?
- ? How does this apply to ______?
- ? What is your hunch (hypothesis, best guess) about this?
- ? Why is this important?
- ? ...
- ? ...

Metacognitive-Level Questions:

- ? Are you sure?
- ? What still needs to be done?
- ? What solutions are emerging?
- ? Where do you see gaps or ambiguities?
- ? Where can we start?
- ? What is your strategy?
- ? How can we fit this together with ______?
- ? Who will do this? By when?
- ? What have you accomplished?
- ? How can we learn more about this?
- ? Have you considered _____ (process or strategy)?
- ? What, if anything, in your goals and strategies need to change?
- ? What conclusions have you drawn?
- ? Have you reached your goal?
- ? How could you go about this?
- ? Why is this (process) important?
- ? What do you want to accomplish?
- ? What obstacles do you see?
- ? What has worked best for you so far?
- ? ...

Epistemic-Level Questions:

- ? How do you know?
- ? Do we need to know more? Why?
- ? What makes you say that?
- ? How will you decide when you know enough to solve this problem?
- ? How will you determine your best solution?
- ? What can we know? To what degree of certainty?
- ? What is at stake here?
- ? If _____, then ______?
- ? How does that relate to our problem statement?
- ? How does your role (perspective) influence your knowing and concerns?

Source: © 1995 Revised 2000. Illinois Mathematics and Science Academy—The Center @ IMSA. Reproduced by permission.

FIGURE 7.4
Questioning Strategies in PBL

Questions are one of our best tools to increase and assess student understanding in PBL. Questions help students think, reflect on their thinking, and consider information and consequences.

The following are some examples of different question types:

? **Probes** ask students to go deeper into an idea or concept, such as: *Can you say more about that?*

? **Challenges** prompt students to support their claims or validate their reasoning, such as: *How do you know that to be true?*

? **Redirects** bring students back to the problem, such as: *Before our discussion you said ____; what do you think now, Jennifer?*

? **Goal-setting prompts** help students set goals for their inquiry and solutions, such as: *Where do you think we can find out that information?*

? **Monitors** encourage students to monitor their inquiry and problem-solving processes, such as: *Do you have everything you need to report out in your group?*

Source: © 2000 Illinois Mathematics and Science Academy—The Center @ IMSA. Adapted by permission.

Assessment *for* Learning. Whether individuals, small groups, or the full class generates problem statements, they provide insight into students' holistic understanding of the problem at hand and a baseline to assess their growing understanding.

Assessment *of* Learning. As students build a holistic understanding of the overarching problem, coaches should convey their expectation that students grasp the situation and elicit written problem statements from each student that include the issue and the conditions necessary for an acceptable resolution.

Iterations of the Investigative Stages of Inquiry

Among the activities that can take place at this stage are know, need to know, and new ideas charting; information gathering and sharing; and refining the problem statement.

Assessment *for* Learning. Are students aware at this point that demographic questions are as important as the science questions?

- Why is plague limited to rural areas?
- Why don't we have epidemics of plague in large cities?
- Are certain groups more susceptible to plague (gender, age, ethnic, income level, lifestyle, etc.)?

Math questions also surface:

- Can we define an epidemic mathematically?
- If there were only 11 cases of plague in the United States in 1988 and 14 in 1993, how can this be an epidemic?

Questions related to other diseases in the area affected and the correlation between these diseases and climatic conditions ultimately emerge.

Assessment *of* Learning. As students gain and apply learning, expectations for production or performance can include:

- Memo to the supervisor of the investigation explaining causal linkages
- Graphs depicting susceptibility of different groups
- Mathematical model of the spread of disease
- Written explanation of the definition and classification of epidemic or plague in response to a question from a reporter
- Concept or "mind mapping" of an individual's or a group's understanding of the problematic situation compared to a map of an expert's view of the situation

Generating Possible Resolutions or Solutions

How are the student-epidemiologists, using the information they found, going to address the questions that the investigation posed?

Assessment *for* Learning. Probe and challenge students' thinking as they generate possibilities:

- Does the proposal take into account the varying stakeholder positions?
- Does this issue fall outside the public's right to know?
- Have students considered the consequences of each potential plan?

- What response would students anticipate, and how might that affect relationships within the community?

Assessment *of* Learning. As students synthesize information and evaluate options, expectations for support over assertion are expected:

- Write a report to the CDC director putting forth and assessing the merits of each possible solution
- Write an impact statement to the appropriate governmental level (mayor, governor, etc.) putting forth and assessing the potential consequences of each possible solution

Presenting the Solution

When students are ready to present the solution, assessment for learning still continues.

Assessment *for* Learning. A viable resolution or solution should stand up to scrutiny, and students should demonstrate understanding in multiple ways—for instance, using the facets of understanding.

- Explain the situation fully from multiple perspectives. What conclusions do students draw about plague among the Native American population?
- Imagine yourself the brother of a victim. What might you consider to be the pros and cons of full-scale public revelation of the situation? Why?

Assessment *of* Learning. As students present a specific solution, expectations for organization, clarity, evidence, and a multiperspective understanding of the situation are high. Among the assessable ways that students can present their information are:

- A presentation that conveys the situation, possible causes, anticipated solution, and potential effects in an organized and articulate manner.
- Responding to the questions of stakeholders and experts in the field. The responses should demonstrate knowledge of evidence and empathy, as well as a depth of knowledge that goes beyond the first, "Why?"
- Stakeholder assessment based upon their interactions with students either in a mentoring capacity or as a member of the panel to whom students present findings.
- Peer assessment based upon a rubric co-constructed by the class members.
- "Letter to the Editor" following the misreporting of a student's statement to the press.

Debriefing the Problem

Even after we complete the reports on the experience, more opportunities for enhancing and evaluating learning are available.

Assessment *for* Learning. Debriefing students' learning process and their knowledge/skill acquisition is a critical and necessary aspect of PBL. Coaches can ask the students:

- Knowing what you know now, would you frame the problem differently?

- Who should hold the ultimate responsibility for deciding disclosure in this situation?
- What benefit or harm is possible here?
- What is the foundational or "big" issue at stake?
- What did you learn academically (science, social science, mathematics, psychology, language arts, cultural issues, political issues, etc.)?
- What can you do now that you didn't think you could do before (skills, self-efficacy, self-directed activity, self-knowledge, interact with public officials, have adults listen to me, etc.)?

Assessment *of* Learning. As students reflect on their learning experience, expectations for specific knowledge and skill acquisition, as well as self-knowledge about learning style and strategies, become clear.

- Identification of specific, discipline-based content and skills are raised to a conscious level.
- As a result of a thorough debriefing, correcting misconceptions, and perhaps targeted instruction at concepts missed or minimized, assessment through traditional written quizzes or exams are potential means for capturing learning data for reporting and decision-making purposes.
- Student self-assessment of learning gain through a rubric co-constructed by classmates.
- Self, peer, and or teacher assessment relative to knowledge and skill gains toward learning standards valued by school and district.

As promised, multiple possibilities—both for and of learning—abound in a problem-based learning experience.

Assessing the Assessors: Success Lab Example

In Chapter 1 we talked about our work with educators to bring PBL into a greater number of classrooms. Another way that we accomplish this coverage is by using PBL in our work with educators and administrators. Remember the question, "How do you know a good one when you see one?" This question is an ideal way to approach educational quality assurance when working with educational supervisors charged with coaching and monitoring the quality of an educational setting (lab, classroom, school, etc).

During the summer of 2000, Success Lab Learning Centers identified the need for a Quality Assurance Program for its 32 centers. Success Lab serves urban, at-risk students in grades K–12 with supplemental, diagnostic reading and mathematics programs housed within its partner schools and park district facilities. The program had experienced tremendous growth recently, and its leaders were aware of the imperative to assess and monitor program quality to assure that they were meeting the needs of learners and partner institutions.

In working with the directors and area managers of Success Lab Centers, we posed the question, "How do you know a good one when you see one?" In essence, assessment itself constituted their ill-structured problem (see Chapter 2 for a definition of an ill-structured problem). This question tested their understanding of the role and function of the centers, as well as the varying aspects of operation,

service to learners, commitment to results, and, ultimately, their reason for being: the vision that all children can learn. Through the events of a PBL learning experience, we coached them through a revealing and rewarding process that clarified in a descriptive way the quality criteria, benchmarks, indicators, and ultimate standards for all Success Lab Learning Centers.

What emerged was a series of six rubrics that not only tested their understanding and capacity in their varying roles, but also provided multiple lenses through which they might "see" each learning center clearly. Figure 7.5 shows one of these descriptive rubrics.

This descriptive rubric serves to focus center operation as it relates to the ethos of the learning environment. What does this mean? Managers use this rubric to provide formative assessment (*for* learning) on a monthly basis. For example, in a lab performing *below expectations*, a tone of staff superiority interferes with learning; in a lab performing *above expectations*, the staff and the children have a feeling of pride and accomplishment in all they do. This same rubric, when transformed into an analytic rubric (see Figure 7.6), provides a tool for quality assurance specialists who visit and observe at each learning center twice a year—one scheduled and one unscheduled visit.

Assessment to Create New Learning: Thinking Log Example

Another important aspect of a problem-based learning experience is the opportunity to delve into a situation for an

Success Lab Learning Centers
Lab Quality Assurance Descriptors—Ethos

	Unacceptable	Below Expectations	Needs Improvement	The SUCCESS LAB Standard	Above Expectations
Tone of the Teaching and Learning Ethos	• Upon entering the lab, a sense of gloom ensues due to poor lighting, negative attitudes, dismal and/or tired decorations, etc.	• A tone of superiority interferes with making a true connection with the students to foster learning.	• The lab exudes a sense of *schoolness*, in that everything is learning-focused—from the instruction, to the tenor of conversation, to the décor, to the interactions of the director with the children.	• The lab exudes a sense of *schoolness*, in that everything is learning-focused—from the instruction, to the tenor of conversation, to the décor, to the interactions of the director with the children. • In addition, the team and the children have a feeling of pride and accomplishment that comes through in all that they do and say.	• The lab exudes a sense of *schoolness*, in that everything is learning-focused—from the instruction, to the tenor of conversation, to the décor, to the interactions of the director with the children. • In addition, the team and the children have a feeling of pride and accomplishment that comes through in all that they do and say.
Focus of the Teaching and Learning Ethos	• The lab is chaotic and loosely structured (if at all). Precious time is lost to the low level of task-focused behavior of both teachers and students.	• The lab runs very mechanically—regimented and precise—not allowing for the flexibility that working with children demands.	• The lab runs automatically (flows)—directed and guided, but all parties feel empowered in their roles.	• The lab runs automatically (flows)—directed and guided, but all parties feel empowered in their roles. • Children reflect an orientation to task commitment and learning.	• The lab runs automatically (flows)—directed and guided, but all parties feel empowered in their roles. • Children reflect an orientation to task commitment and learning. • Opportunities abound that enable teachers to take advantage of those "teachable moments" that have high impact.
Beliefs Signaled by the Teaching and Learning Ethos	• A general belief exists that these students **cannot** learn.	• Not everyone believes that all children can learn, as evidenced by negative or sarcastic comments.	• A general belief exists that these students can learn, as evidenced by sincere and positively focused interactions.	• A substantial belief, based on caring and experience, exists that the students can learn. • Interactions with students in learning situations reflect knowledge of best practices and relevant research that contributes to a comfort level with instruction.	• The lab environment and interactions signal a level of respect for the children and each other, as well as a sincere belief that all children can learn. • Interactions with students in learning situations reflect knowledge of best practices and relevant research that contributes to a comfort level with instruction.

FIGURE 7.6
Analytic Rubric for a Learning Center

Success Lab Learning Centers
Lab Quality Assurance Descriptors—Ethos

QA/Ethos	Tone	Focus	Beliefs Signaled	Total	Overall %
Center "XYZ"	/5	/5	/5	/15	

Success Lab Learning Center: ______________________ Center Director: ______________________

QA Visit Date & Time: ______________________ Area Manager: ______________________

Director and/or Manager Comments: ______________________

____

____

____

____

This assessment and any comments noted above have been discussed with the Quality Assurance Specialist. Signatures **do not** signify agreement, but rather awareness of the assessment, comments, and follow-up necessary as detailed on attached.

SL Director: ______________________ Date: __________ Follow-up Date(s): ______________________

SL Manager: ______________________ Date: __________ Follow-up Date(s): ______________________

QA Specialist: ______________________ Date: __________ Follow-up Date(s): ______________________

Source: © 2000 Success Lab Learning Centers, Chicago, IL. Reproduced by permission.

FIGURE 7.7
Thinking Log Grading Rubric

Characteristics of *A* Journals

- In-depth and frequent entries.
- Evidence of both directed and nondirected entries. *Directed writing* means those assignments made specifically by the teacher; in *nondirected* and frequently important types of entries, the student is motivated by the desire and need to write. These nondirected topics are not just for the topic at hand.
- Evidence of a great deal of risk taking with thinking shows that the thinker is willing to try out ideas and syntheses of ideas.
- Often neat, polished, or "finished." This presentation demonstrates a habit of thinking that is reflected in the pride of workmanship. There may be unpolished and, at times, cryptic entries, but the good journal writer frequently visits the journal to "put it in order."
- A conscious attempt to pay attention to spelling and writing mechanics.

Characteristics of *B* Journals

- Evidence of both directed and nondirected entries, but more teacher-directed writing. The difference between an *A* journal and a *B* journal is that the *A* journal shows strong self-motivation and the willingness to "go the extra mile."
- Less interest in taking risks with thinking. These journal writers sometimes seem to go for the minimum expectations to receive the decent grade. *B* journals frequently prompt the teacher to comment, "not enough depth"; "needs more analysis"; or "you have to cultivate the habit of writing more frequently." Writing frequently and more in-depth begets more ideas and insights.
- Evidence that the writer doesn't revisit his/her writing to give it polish and finish.

Characteristics of *C* Journals

- Little or no nondirected writing and very little directed writing.
- Shallow thinking or not enough writing to help the teacher judge. The writer seems to say, "From what I have given you, figure out what I do or do not know."
- Anger or a claim that the writer doesn't know what to write.
- Little or no risk-taking with thinking—or none that is documented.
- Little attempt to synthesize what the student is learning—much less thinking.
- Sloppy, indicating a habit of mind that shows little concern about the writer's respect for his or her own thinking and writing.

Characteristics of *D* Journals

- Always turned in late.
- Contains only a few scribbles or comments from the "Ozone Level."
- Documentation of the students' thinking is flawed or absent. Learners seem to be indifferent to their own thinking.

Source: © 1998 by B.C. Hollister, Illinois Mathematics and Science Academy. Adapted by permission.

extended time period and think about it as one is learning more about it—and then transforming what is known in a conscious and conscientious manner to new learning. Bernie Hollister, creator of the plague problem, applied what he called "Thinking Logs" to capture his students' thinking and make it visible (and coachable). In his highly interactive class discussions, he probed, questioned, and challenged his students to think. Using their Thinking Logs, they shared their thoughts, arguments, and puzzles, growing and learning and becoming thinkers under his expert guidance. Bernie graded these journals (with letter grades A, B, C, D) using the rubric in Figure 7.7—holding all his students accountable to benchmarks of good thinking. For example, a D journal contains only a few scribbles or comments, whereas an A journal contains in-depth and frequent entries.

Final Thoughts

Although assessment possibilities exist at every turn in a problem-based learning experience, our overarching goal is to *engage students in thinking*: sustained thinking about and grappling with a problematic situation. In doing so, they are accessing prior knowledge, applying knowledge and skills learned in and out of school, and learning within a meaningful context. The research on PBL shows that students who can sustain thought and bring in a variety of perspectives to their approach to learning will have longer-lasting results from their learning experiences. They will emerge better able to meet the challenges awaiting them, whatever their future pursuits may be.

8

How Do You Support Problem-Based Learning?

THIS CHAPTER EXAMINES ISSUES RELATED TO DEVELOPING a PBL initiative—large or small—in your school, university, or community. Many stakeholders are involved in a decision to use PBL—teacher, student, principal, department chair, curriculum coordinator, superintendent or chancellor, parent, or business or community partner. We address concerns or questions such stakeholders often have about PBL.

Why PBL?

John Abbott (1996) makes a strong argument for what he calls the "new competencies"—skills that go far beyond the 19th century basics taught in many schools. The "old competencies" of numeracy, literacy, calculation, and communication are still necessary to function in modern society; but they are not enough. For success in our ever-changing world, the ability to conceptualize problems and solutions is essential. Abbott asserts that the new competencies that must be nurtured and developed include the following:

- **Abstraction.** The mental manipulation of thoughts and patterns in a purposive and ongoing manner.
- **Systems thinking.** The ability to see the interrelatedness of things and the effect of parts upon the whole and the whole upon parts.
- **Experimentation.** The questioning frame of mind that encourages hypothesizing, testing, and evaluating data.
- **Collaboration.** The disposition to be open-minded and adaptable as we coconstruct knowledge together.

These competencies parallel the call for workplace know-how highlighted by the Secretary's Commission for Achieving Necessary Skills (SCANS) (U.S. Department of Labor, 1991). Built on a foundation of basic skills, thinking skills, and personal qualities, the SCANS competencies include the following:

- **Resources.** Allocating time, money, and materials.
- **Interpersonal skills.** Working on teams, leading others, negotiating, and showing tolerance.
- **Information.** Acquiring, organizing, evaluating, and interpreting data.
- **Systems.** Understanding social, organizational, and technological systems.
- **Technology.** Selecting and applying technology appropriately.

PBL classrooms are learning communities where information and the construction of knowledge are collective activities. Students who gather, share, and add information to the knowledge pool assess the information for validity and integrate it as appropriate. Expertise grows among community members through dialogue, jigsaw, questioning, reciprocal teaching, and mentoring. Individual learners must then synthesize this knowledge into a holistic understanding of the problem at hand.

"Teaching for understanding" is a phrase heard frequently today in education, but student understanding is an elusive thing to define, let alone capture. Rebecca Simmons (1994), project manager for the Teaching for Understanding Project at Harvard, describes understanding in this way:

> We want students to be able to employ knowledge in flexible and novel ways, to develop flexible networks of concepts, to use what they learn in school to understand the world around them, and to develop interest in lifelong intellectual pursuits. But to help students achieve such understanding is no mean feat. (p. 22)

Diann Musial and Liz Hammerman (1997) of Northern Illinois University describe the intimate perspective of PBL learners:

> The problem-based learner tends to develop mental patterns that are highly connected to the richness of the problem situation. Such understanding is highly integrated and linked to a variety of real-world situations, perspectives, disciplines, etc. Such learners are able to

answer essay questions not only in terms of the definition of terms; they are able to elaborate on the meaning of important ideas and add nuances that are connected to the real world. This is so, *not* because they have read about those connections, but because they have experienced the connections firsthand. (p. 6) (emphasis in original)

The challenge of higher education in the face of an information explosion, as well as the demands of the high-performance workplace, has clearly established a need to prepare our students for an increasingly complex environment. Problem solving and the higher-order thinking skills of analysis, synthesis, and evaluation are not learned through direct instruction. They emerge from the direct experience of doing. PBL provides that experience.

How Do We Know That PBL Works?

PBL has a rich history in professional schools (medical, dental, nursing, engineering, and business) going back decades. Research conducted to assess the effectiveness of PBL programs cites certain benefits, including increased motivation, sustained self-directed learning behaviors, long-term knowledge retention, comparable content coverage with traditional approaches, learning for understanding, and the development of professional reasoning strategies (Albanese & Mitchell, 1993; Eck & Mathews, 2000; Hendley, 1996; Vernon & Blake, 1993). Although interesting, this research is not what K–16 teachers, administrators, and parents want to know. Their bottom-line question, "Will it work for *my* students?" is one that in the end they must answer for themselves.

PBL has been used at the K–16 levels for several years. Anecdotal evidence is highly supportive. Teachers consistently report increased student engagement in the learning process, increased student responsibility for learning, and deeper levels of understanding. Library and media specialists report that students use more library materials, develop effective search strategies, and gain in information literacy. Principals report that discipline referrals and absenteeism decrease. Parents report hearing about what is happening at school *without having to ask*.

In today's educational climate, one key concern is *to do no harm*. Two middle grade teachers, Karoline Krynock and Louise Robb (1996), investigated a perennial question posed about any educational innovation: Can students gain the same or greater depth and breadth of knowledge through a problem-based unit as through a standard unit? In a rigorous study, they compared four sections of science classes—two standard, two PBL—on content achievement in a genetics unit in the 8th grade curriculum. Teaching strategies and the curriculum organization differed, but the content was identical. The researchers used and scored a common instrument to assess content achievement or attainment. These results were compared against district-administered standardized test scores aggregated by class. All four classes were directly comparable on this standardized measure of intellectual ability, but the *PBL classes scored slightly higher on the genetics content assessment.*

The PBL classes were assigned to research a messy, ill-structured problem and provide evidence to support their conclusions. They had to write a persuasive position paper and present their conclusions before a panel of professionals knowledgeable in the field of behavioral genetics. During the problem debriefing, students went beyond the testable material and reported that they learned how to do the following:

- Investigate a complex issue.
- Collaborate with peers as learning colleagues in groups.
- Look beyond print material for information and contact experts directly.
- Present their information to a panel of experts.
- Take a position and defend their conclusions using data.
- Think about multiple solutions instead of jumping to conclusions.

Although this study was well done and is highly regarded (winner of a state-level research award), the important issues here go beyond the study results. These educators are not only able to describe their program clearly to parents, students, and administrators, but also to answer the deeper questions of *What works?* and *How do we know?*

Richard Dods (1996), a science/chemistry teacher, writes:

> Although process is emphasized [in PBL], content is not lost. Ongoing action research studies [in his course] compare students who have experienced PBL biochemistry with those who have experienced biochemistry in an interactive questioning format. Results suggest that the PBL biochemistry approach promotes deeper understanding of biochemical content and longer-term recall of content than the interactive questioning format. (p. 228)

Dods believes that a student's "problem-based frame of mind" provides a web of understanding that meaningfully connects individual pieces of content. These connections enable access and recall through multiple avenues that support deeper levels of understanding.

What About PBL and Standards?

Although some educators (e.g., Kanstoroom & Finn, 1999) believe that constructivist educational methods fly in the face of academic standards, we do not find common sense in that argument. We find the key to achieving standards for all students comes not in restricting *how* teachers teach, but in setting common goals for students. Constructivist and traditional classroom structures may both be used toward this end:

> State and local curriculums address *what* students learn. Constructivism, as an approach to education, addresses *how* students learn. The constructivist teacher, in mediating students' learning, blends the *what* with the *how*. (Brooks, M. G., and Brooks, 1999, p. 22) (emphasis in original)

Standards can help set benchmarks for students at various levels and encourage high expectations for all students (Glickman, 2000). However, standards can also artificially narrow the range of knowledge, skills, and dispositions we expect from students of various ages. One of the greatest difficulties comes when measurement of student progress toward standards comes from just a single test score, often the state standardized test (Glickman, 2000; Kohn, 2000). Certainly most standardized tests are not designed to assess many of the documented benefits of PBL, like self-directed learning, critical thinking, integrative knowledge, and so on. We are convinced that, as states implement their academic standards, evidence will show that strategies like PBL are even more supportive of achievement than lecture, discussion, and worksheets. This connection is already provable in medical education. We are not convinced, however, that any single measurement—particularly standardized tests—shows the added benefits students gain from PBL.

That said, we understand that teachers across the United States must demonstrate alignment of their curriculum and instruction with standards. When we work with teachers to design problems, we begin with learner characteristics and desired curriculum outcomes. In effect, teachers design PBL experiences around specific standards.

In a middle school class (Sage, Krynock, & Robb, 2000), the teachers aligned their PBL unit with several student and teacher science standards. The problem, examining what should be done with improperly maintained prairie areas on the school campus, enabled students to achieve several national science standards, including:

By the end of 8th grade, students should know that . . . in any particular environment, the growth and survival of organisms depends on the physical conditions. (American Association for the Advancement of Science, AAAS, Project 2061, 1993, p. 117)

By the end of 8th grade, students should:
• Question claims based on vague attributions.
• Notice and criticize the reasoning in arguments in which fact and opinion are intermingled. (AAAS, 1993, p. 299)

The two teachers' work in this interdisciplinary, problem-based English and science class correlates with one of the National Research Council's (1996) standards for teachers:

[Teachers] work together as colleagues within and across disciplines and grade levels. . . . Teachers of science guide and facilitate learning. In doing this, teachers focus and support inquiries while interacting with students. (p. 32)

Using PBL in mathematics aligns beautifully with the National Council of Teachers of Mathematics (NCTM) (2000) standards for students and teachers, as well (e.g., Alper, Fendel, Fraser, & Resek, 1996; Erickson, 1999; Sage, Kochanowski, & Shafii-Mousavi, 2001). One of the NCTM standards is problem solving. Teachers are encouraged to help students build the disposition to be analytic and persistent in complex situations. They can do this work by "asking questions that help students find the mathematics in their worlds and experiences and by encouraging students to persist with interesting but challenging problems" (NCTM, 2000, p. 52). Sounds like PBL! Here is an example of a brief PBL experience from the NCTM (2000) standards:

A task for middle-grades students presents data about two ambulance companies and asks which company is more reliable. . . . A quick answer found by looking at the average time customers had to wait for each company turns out to be misleading. A more careful mathematical analysis involving plotting response times versus time of day reveals a different solution. (p. 52)

Standards in the humanities are readily accomplished using PBL as well. One example is Indiana's 10th grade reading comprehension standard #2 (Indiana State Board of Education, 2000, p. 2):

> Analyze the structure and format of various informational documents and explain how authors use the features to achieve their purposes.

> *Example:* Analyze an advertisement that has been made to look like the informational newspaper or magazine text around it. Explain why the advertisement would be designed this way and evaluate its effectiveness.

This scenario could easily become PBL, perhaps by placing students in the role of advertising teams designing an ad campaign for a new drug targeted at senior citizens. In creating their various advertisements, students would look at other similar ads in which the above structure is used. They would have to weigh the ethics of such an approach as they design their own ads.

In the National Standards for Social Studies Teachers (National Council for the Social Studies [NCSS], 1997), as one example, teachers of young children are encouraged to meet standards in Strand VI (Power, Authority, and Governance) by exploring the current governance structures in their school. One kindergarten teacher we worked with aligned a problem with this standard by encouraging students to examine the current lost and found policy in their school to see how efficient, equitable, and fair it was. She knew this problem would be appropriate early in the year because kindergarten students often lose their belongings! They presented their findings to the principal, who changed the policy accordingly.

What About PBL and Technology?

In addition to the standards mentioned, schools are implementing local and national technology standards (see, for example, the National Educational Technology Standards for Students [International Society for Technology in Education, 2000]). PBL is a natural fit for helping students meet technology standards (Sage, 2000a). Technology is critical to PBL in several ways. It can be used as a tool and resource for inquiry, as a collaboration aid, as curriculum, and as assessment. Figure 8.1 gives examples.

First, sources like the Internet and online reference materials are invaluable when students are researching a problem. For example, students can access demographic information on any county in the United States from the U.S. Census Bureau Web site (www.census.gov). This information is important for a number of different kinds of problems. Internet and online resources are often helpful,

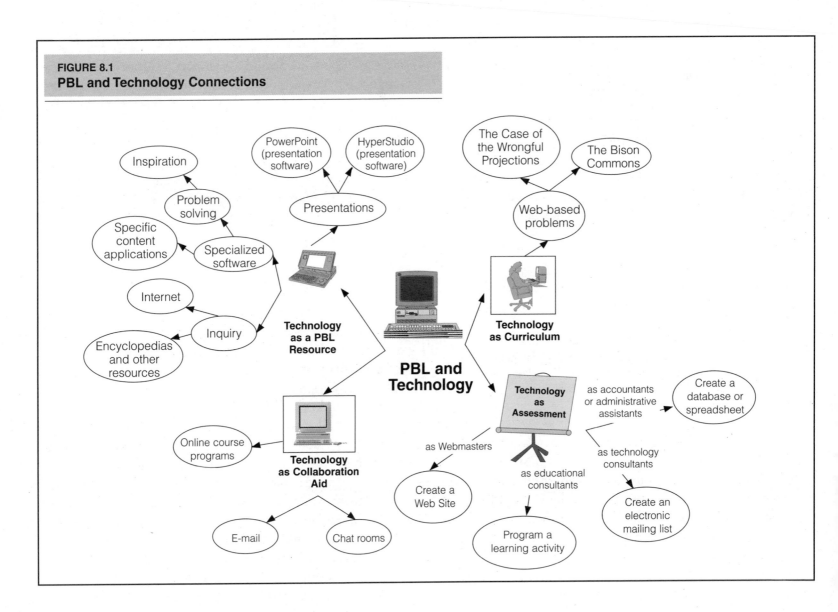

FIGURE 8.1
PBL and Technology Connections

graphics-oriented resources during PBL inquiry for non-readers, beginning readers, or ESL students. In its work with low-achieving urban students, Success Lab Learning Centers (Torp, 2000) use authentic Web-based data and expository information about topics of interest to these particular students—chewing gum, ice cream, sporting event statistics, athletic performance, local heroes, and current events—as the organizing focus for PBL work that targets study, research, and information literacy skills. In addition, Stepien, Senn, and Stepien (2000) have developed a number of problem-based learning units that specifically incorporate Internet resources.

Specific software can also help students in their problem-solving work. One of our favorites is Inspiration (www.inspiration.com), which was used to develop a number of the maps and webs in this book. Students can use such visual organizer software to "map" their growing and changing understanding of a problem. Teachers could use students' pre- and post-maps of a problem as one form of assessment. Teachers can also use Inspiration while designing problems to create maps of possibility, as discussed in Chapter 5. Specialized software related to particular discipline-based concepts (such as RAMAS EcoLab, which John Thompson used to model predator-prey dynamics during the wolf problem described in Chapter 6) may be used as one form of instruction during problem solving. Students may also use presentation software such as PowerPoint or HyperStudio to display their results to an expert panel.

Second, increasing numbers of Web-based problems may be appropriate curriculum for your students. One Web site for such problems is the Center for Problem-Based Learning at the Illinois Mathematics and Science Academy (www.imsa.edu/team/cpbl). Several Web-based problems suitable for middle and high school students are available there, including The Case of the Wrongful Projections developed by Bernard C. Hollister (www.imsa.edu/team/cpbl/learning/lincoln/Bernie1-FS.html), which presents students with the dilemma of President Lincoln's incorrect U.S. population projections for the 20th century. Another problem available there is the Buffalo Commons problem (www.imsa.edu/team/cpbl/learning/buffalo). This PBL problem guides students, who are role-playing members of a presidential commission, to a number of Web sites that help them consider whether or not land in the central plains should be deprivatized for use as a buffalo commons. The Appendix lists other sites with Web-based problems.

Third, technology may be used as assessment in PBL. For example, students in a technology course can assume the role of course designers to create a computer-based learning program. Students could, as technology consultants, set up and monitor an e-mail listserver or Web site on a particular issue. The opportunities for classroom teachers and technology specialists to collaborate on problems that delve into both academic content issues and authentic technology use are endless!

Finally, online course programs allow for many collaboration options with PBL. Programs such as Oncourse (http://oncourse.indiana.edu) allow teachers to post documents, schedules, and syllabi online, as well as to set up small-group asynchronous discussions or chat rooms. These online group structures are particularly helpful for PBL when groups need time to problem-solve outside of class. In one recent instructional technology course at Indiana University, students used a previously developed online course tool in a challenging PBL unit learned and taught completely online (Orrill, 2000; Sage, 2000b). Although we personally believe such programs will not, and should not, ever completely replace face-to-face classes and in-person coaching, they allow numerous opportunities for teachers to post questions and information online and for students to have more opportunities for group dialogue.

What Are the Potential Barriers to PBL Adoption?

We find that most educators with whom we work recognize the importance of PBL to increase student motivation to deeper levels of understanding. Yet the "coverage" mantra still dominates many areas, often because our major evaluation instruments drive curriculum choices. Many teachers face restrictive schedules or other structures that work against the time necessary for student engagement and teaching for understanding. Teachers also express frustration with a lack of time during the school day for designing new problems.

Educators also fear change because of school norms that perpetuate the status quo. Some teachers feel they are out on a limb using PBL in their classes. As one middle school teacher reported overhearing another teacher say, "Where

are the worksheets? Where are the tests? . . . They [students] are laughing, they're having fun, they're running around wanting to do research; what is this?"

Teachers and teaching teams who recognize any or all of these obstacles within their schools work proactively to build and nurture support among colleagues and community. Many have enlisted parents as both allies and resources for PBL units. Others tap the knowledge and expertise of school colleagues to serve as mentors in problem inquiries. Although innovation and change can ignite fears and create barriers, communication and openness reveal unseen possibilities. Here are examples of ways to communicate (Sage, Krynock, & Robb, 2000):

- Explaining PBL and providing resources for various stakeholders (see the following section, "How Can I Explain PBL to Parents and the Community?").
- Clearly aligning PBL experiences with standards (see the previous section, "What About PBL and Standards?").
- Designing problems carefully to consider students' developmental characteristics, interests, and issues (e.g., Beane, 1993), so that students are engaged and effective problem-solvers.
- Providing appropriate support for students new to PBL so they have a successful learning experience.
- Debriefing with students and parents after a PBL experience about what students have learned. (Several teachers we know use their class newsletter or the school newsletter to share information both about the problem itself and what students have learned, including specific learning objectives and standards.)

- Involving as many stakeholders as possible in the PBL process (see the following section, "How Can I Explain PBL to Parents and the Community?").
- Locating a support system of like-minded PBL teachers and schools (see Appendix).

Another essential component is support from administrators—support for PBL as well as support provided through resources and assistance with accessing appropriate information. We find most principals eager to support innovations that enhance student learning.

How Can I Explain PBL to Parents and the Community?

PBL may be very different from the instruction that many of us experienced in our own schooling. In our current standards and testing culture, some parents and community members may have concerns about teachers and schools deviating from more traditional methods of instruction. We have consistently found, however, that parents, administrators, school board members, and community members are impressed when they learn more about PBL, particularly if they have the opportunity to observe students at work.

Encouraging these stakeholders to be involved in PBL as guest speakers with expertise on the problem topic, or as members of a panel to which students present their solutions, can be powerful ways to engender community understanding and support for PBL. Nearly always, adults are impressed with the seriousness with which students approach the problem, with their knowledge, and with the entire PBL philosophy. Community members we've worked with believe that K–12 schools and undergraduate institutions should be doing more of this type of instruction to prepare students for their eventual place in an information-driven, problem-centered, collaborative work world.

Several simple sentences that may help you share PBL with people totally unfamiliar with the approach are given here:

- "PBL makes school learning more like real-world learning."
- "PBL helps students learn the same content—just in a different way."
- "Besides learning content, PBL has additional valuable components like helping learners collaborate, problem-solve, make presentations, and talk with experts—many of the things they'll be doing as adults."
- "PBL motivates many students to dig deeper and get 'hooked' into issues; they may actually want to go to the library or go online to get more information!"
- "Think about the times in your life when you have really learned something. Often this learning is related to a problem you were facing. The PBL approach encourages students to learn because they want or need to solve a problem, too."
- "Students don't ask, 'Why do I need to know this?' in PBL. The answer is clear: They need to know it to solve the problem."

Schools now have a number of resources available for sharing within their communities information about PBL. This book and others (e.g., Delisle, 1997) are rich resources for people who want detailed information. ASCD also has the helpful Problem-Based Learning Series (Association for Supervision and Curriculum Development, 1997), which includes two videos with a facilitator guide. Another excellent video is *Problem-Based Learning: Three Classrooms in Action* (Center for Problem-Based Learning, 1997), available from the Center for Problem-Based Learning at the Illinois Mathematics and Science Academy (http://www.imsa.edu/team/cpbl/products/videos.html).

What Does It Take to Become a Teacher of PBL?

We have found that PBL requires a facility to use a coaching style that preservice and inservice experiences often do not address. As an ongoing part of our professional development activities, we asked teachers to reflect on what they were learning about teaching PBL (Sage & Torp, 1997) and concluded the following:

- **Making the transition from teacher as information-giver to teacher as coach is challenging and requires learning new skills.** Teachers discussed giving up the idea that they had to be the experts. Some found it difficult to let go of the sense of control and predictability typical in more traditional instruction; eventually most teachers came to realize that, as a

middle school teacher put it, "Not only do I need to let go, I need to stay there [to provide support to students]." Teachers also learned in their role as coach how to question students' thinking and to challenge students to support their conclusions. One staff development coordinator said, "We learned that we needed to focus our language on the language of *thinking*."

- **Designing problem scenarios requires a sound understanding of problem-based learning, curriculum, and authentic assessment.** Teachers wrestled with the design of problem scenarios as they worked to integrate required curriculum outcomes and incorporate the teaching and assessment of meaningful skills throughout the problem. Considering *what* content their problems would address also challenged teachers to consider essential knowledge of disciplines rather than automatically using textbook-defined content. As teachers designed assessments, they had to consider how to use them so that the assessment measured student thinking and guided, but did not limit, learning. Teachers also found they were teaching skills, such as writing business letters, in more authentic ways—that is, teaching in the context of the problem rather than in isolation.

- **Learning in a PBL environment is exciting for students and rewarding for teachers.** Teachers found that seeing what students could do led them to *trust* their students more. Lisa Nicholson, a special education instructor, said, "PBL has proven to me that if you don't give the kids limitations and if you overlook their disabilities, PBL gives them the chance to learn the way they need to learn." Teachers believed that because PBL encourages students to explore information in different ways—such as through print, telephone, and the Internet—and to learn about authentic problems, PBL was also a motivating strategy for students with varied learning styles and strengths.

We have discovered that teachers of PBL benefit from multiple supports, including active support in their schools from administrators and other teachers. Team teaching has been an effective method of support. If other teachers in the building are not implementing PBL, then teachers need a network of other practitioners with whom to share ideas and find help. The Center for Problem-Based Learning has established such a network for teachers as well as an electronic mail list (see Appendix). This networking is particularly critical for more experienced PBL practitioners to communicate with others who have similar concerns (Gibbons, 1995).

We have found that teachers don't always fully buy in to PBL, particularly to their role as coaches, until they've tried it and seen how powerful the experience is for their students. Teachers find it particularly helpful to see as many examples as possible of PBL problems other teachers at their level have designed and implemented. We have also found that *using* PBL to *teach* PBL is essential, so that teachers experience PBL as learners first (Sage & Torp, 1997; Sage, 2001). Like any effective learning experience for students, teachers also benefit from a collaborative climate of learning challenges and appropriate support (see Figure 8.2).

In Closing

For PBL practitioners, PBL's effectiveness is unquestionable. These educators point to many positive effects:

- Students turned off by more traditional approaches emerge as active, engaged learners.
- Students can talk about a topic in depth—not simply answer factual questions.
- Students ask for targeted lessons about what they need to know to solve a problem.
- Students ask good questions that reflect an understanding deeper than any response shows.
- Students know how to locate, evaluate, and use information effectively.
- And, of course, students learn and perform well on content tests.

Problem-based learning has been used in urban and rural settings; with elementary, secondary, college-level, and professional students; with reluctant learners; and with eager learners—in short, with students of all abilities and ages in almost every subject area. PBL consistently receives high marks from students, parents, and administrators whenever the teacher is motivated and well versed in PBL techniques. PBL exposes solid, demanding content; engages students at an emotional level; and fosters skills needed in a complex world. Teachers can use PBL as a curriculum organizer and instructional strategy whenever learning goals demand deeper understandings—whether occasionally or frequently—in tandem with other strategies. We believe PBL is a powerful technique that all teachers should have in their repertoire for the 21st century.

FIGURE 8.2
The PBL Environment: Concerns, Challenges, and Support

Balancing Professional Challenges
With Appropriate Support

Fundamental Concerns That Drive PBL Professional Development

Challenges

Support

- What is my role as teacher/coach in PBL?

- What new skills do I need?

- How should we prepare students as citizens in tomorrow's world?

- What knowledge is most critical?

- How do we assess student learning in PBL?

- How do we communicate effectively about PBL to others?

	Challenges	Support
Context	• Philosophical differences within school community • Isolation from professional peers • Questionable level of administrative support • Tentative parent/community relations	• Appropriate resources • Teaming with colleagues • Active administrative backing • Electronic network to facilitate dialogue across sites and across professional contexts
Teaching	• Integrating complex understandings • Adopting new practices • Assuming a new role • Modifying grounding beliefs • Modulating concerns	• Appropriate information when needed • Collegial dialogue • Modeling by experienced coaches • Practice in a safe environment • Mentoring by PBL practitioners
Learning	• Creating authentic learning situations that address standards • Integrating content and process • Coaching and managing active student learning • Capturing the effects of PBL teaching and learning	• Clear learning expectations • Practice and mentoring • Evidence of student learning and growth • Collegial network of PBL practitioners

Adapted from Torp & Sage (1998), p. 89. © 1997 Illinois Mathematics and Science Academy, Center for Problem-Based Learning, Aurora, IL.

Appendix

How Can I Learn More About Problem-Based Learning?

I. ASCD Member Network

The Problem-Based Learning Network (PBL Net) is one of ASCD's member networks. Our goal is to create a strong base of support for problem-based learning among educators at all levels. Problem-based learning enhances understanding through more relevant, connected learning and taps students' natural curiosity about the world around them to ignite motivation for learning. Students address issues that challenge them to apply what they have learned in authentic ways.

PBL Net maintains and supports an interpersonal and electronic network to enable dialogue and the sharing of information, methods, and materials. We strive to enhance our understanding of problem-based learning from the perspectives of learner, coach, and problem designer.

Our award-winning newsletter, *The Problem Log*, connects and inspires our members. Acknowledged experts in PBL submit articles, as do practitioners eager to share classroom experiences. Reflections of teachers in the midst of changing teaching and learning in their classrooms, reports of teachers' action research related to PBL, and dissemination of relevant research about PBL (K–16) round out each issue.

Member fees are $15 per year, due on the anniversary of initial membership. Members receive three issues of *The Problem Log* annually. PBL Net holds an annual meeting and discussion forum scheduled concurrently with the ASCD Annual Conference.

For membership information contact: The Center @IMSA, Illinois Mathematics and Science Academy, 1500 W. Sullivan Road, Aurora, IL 60506; or e-mail: pbl-info@ imsa.edu; or call 630-907-5956 or 630-907-5957.

II. Electronic Mailing List

An electronic mailing list (IMSACPBL-L) facilitates online dialogue among those interested and working in problem-based learning. The Illinois Mathematics and Science Acad-

emy maintains this list, which is made possible through additional funding provided by The Hitachi Foundation.

To subscribe:
Send mail to: MAJORDOMO@IMSA.EDU
With the message: subscribe imsacpbl-l [your e-mail address]

To send mail:
Send mail to: IMSACPBL-L@IMSA.EDU

To get more information about using the list:
Send mail to: MAJORDOMO@IMSA.EDU
With the message: HELP

III. Threaded Discussion Forum

The Center@IMSA also moderates a threaded discussion forum on ASCD's WWW site: http://www.ascd.org/forums.html. Click on ASCD Network: Problem-Based Learning. Add your thoughts and comments to the ongoing discussion.

IV. World Wide Web Sites

1. The Carnegie Foundation site gives a description of a teacher education problem.
http://kml.carnegiefoundation.org/gallery/bcerbin/Course_Overview/MSS_Problem/mss_problem.html

2. The Center@IMSA address is http://www.imsa.edu/ center/. Click on CPBL. You may also access the Center for Problem-Based Learning directly at http://www.imsa.edu/ team/cpbl/cpbl.html. This site remains the best for PBL at

K–16 and provides information related to the following key questions:

- What is the Center for Problem-Based Learning?
- What is problem-based learning (PBL)?
- What does PBL look like in the classroom?
- Who is doing PBL?
- Who can I contact to learn more?

The site also includes two WWW-based interactive PBL problems:

- The Bison Commons. An interactive WWW-based PBL problem for middle grade and high school students, complete with problem information links and a Teacher Information Center.
- SUPERLAND! A WWW-based PBL problem used in the Summer AD'Ventures program for middle grade students, complete with individual student products.

3. The Center for Advanced Research and Technology's site describes a project-based high school in California: http://www.cart.org

4. The El Dorado County Office of Education site hosts several K–12 problems: http://www.edcoe.k12.ca.us/tech/pbl.html

5. The Learning Tree of San Diego State University site: http://edweb.sdsu.edu/clrit/learningtree/Ltree.html

6. The Library of Congress's Learning Page contains two WWW-based interactive PBL problems known as the Reservation Controversies Scenarios.

http://memory. loc.gov/ammem/ndlpedu/lessons/97/reservation/teacher.html

7. NASA's Classroom of the Future at the Center for Educational Technology at Wheeling Jesuit University is host to an array of problem-based and project-based possibilities. The center's work in the design, development, and research of innovative educational strategies—including PBL—is commendable: http://www.cotf.edu/

8. PROBLARC, the Australian Problem-Based Learning Center: http://www.newcastle.edu.au/services/iesd/learndevelop/problarc/

9. Samford University's site provides notes from the PBL 2000 Conference and information on submitting PBL course portfolios for the National Peer Review Project (PBL-PR). Although the focus is on undergraduate education, the site is certainly helpful to all: http://www.samford.edu/pbl

10. The UBUYACAR PBL online experience was developed by the Maricopa Center for Learning and Instruction of Maricopa Community College: http://www.mcli.dist.maricopa.edu/pbl/ubuytutor/index.html

11. The University of Delaware site has articles and sample problems geared to the undergraduate level: http://www.udel.edu/pbl

V. The Center for the Advancement and Renewal of Learning and Teaching— The Center@IMSA

The Illinois Mathematics and Science Academy (IMSA) is an educational laboratory for designing and testing innovative programs and methods to share with other teachers and schools in Illinois and beyond. Included in the laboratory is a three-year (grades 10–12) residential program for Illinois students talented in mathematics and science.

The Academy's mission is "to transform mathematics and science teaching and learning by developing ethical leaders who know the joy of discovering and forging connections within and among mathematics, science, the arts, and the humanities by means of an exemplary laboratory environment characterized by innovative teaching, research, and service."

To advance IMSA's mission, the Academy established the Center for Problem-Based Learning in 1992. In 1998 the Center for Problem-Based Learning became an integral part of the Center for the Advancement and Renewal of Learning and Teaching—the Center@IMSA. The center engages in PBL professional development, curriculum development, research, information exchange, and networking in K–16 educational settings. Here are its goals:

- To mentor educators in all disciplines as they design and develop effective problem-based learning materials and become skillful coaches.
- To explore problem-based learning strategies as the context in which knowledge is acquired, ethical de-

cision making is nurtured, and problem-solving skills are developed.
- To connect problem-based learning educators through numerous networking options designed to meet a variety of needs.

VI. PBL Curriculum Possibilities

The Center for Educational Technologies (CET) develops K–12 curriculum supplements that combine innovative teaching methods with technology tools and real-world problems. The supplements feature

- Hands-on experimentation.
- Observation, collection, analysis, and interpretation of data.
- Cooperative learning and collaboration with experts.
- Problem-based learning.
- Use of mathematics, science, and technology education in an integrated manner.
- Scientific inquiry and critical consideration of competing hypotheses.
- Presentation of hypotheses, method, and results.

The content for these curriculum supplements has been drawn from, but is not limited to, the following subject areas:

- Space sciences and earth system science.
- Life science and biology.
- Physical sciences.
- Environmental sciences.
- Social studies and geography.

- Chemistry and physics.
- Astronomy and mathematics.
- Technology and humanities.

Astronomy Village: Investigating the Solar System
Currently under development at the CWT, this will be a CD-ROM-based multimedia approach to the solar system. The project is funded by the National Science Foundation.

Astronomy Village: Investigating the Universe
This Macintosh CD-ROM-based multimedia program provides 9th and 10th grade science classrooms with 10 complete investigations in stellar astronomy.

BioBLAST
This CD-ROM makes use of 3-D virtual reality technologies and introduces students to NASA research aimed at long-term space habitation.

Exploring the Environment
Students work online with 17 Web-based learning modules that address real environmental dilemmas worldwide.

ExoQuest
This CD-ROM–based multimedia curriculum supplement for grades 7–9 provides an interdisciplinary approach to understanding.

Space Station Challenge
This WWW-based curriculum supplement is for students in grades 9–12. The activities immerse students in standards-based mathematics, science, and technology design and construction projects.

American Memory Learning Page
The Library of Congress's American Memory Learning Page contains many creative ideas in teacher-created and classroom-tested lessons. Photographs from the American Memory collection, "America from the Great Depression to World War II," can be used to teach the novel, *Jacob Have I Loved*. This idea is just one of many creative approaches provided. Lessons can be found at:

http://memory.loc.gov/ammem/ndlpedu/lessons/index.html

Two of these ideas are WWW-based interactive PBL problems known as the Reservation Controversies Scenarios found at:

http://memory.loc.gov/ammem/ndlpedu/lessons/97/reservation/teacher.html

- *The Indian Agent Appointment Interview*. This scenario places the student in 1873 as an Indian agent for the Comanche Indian reservation. The unit provides selected online links and resources. A *prompt* initiates the problem.
- *The Indian Reservation Gaming Issue*. This scenario is placed in the present. The student takes the role of a newly appointed congressional intern who has received a letter from the his congresswoman asking for help regarding issues about gaming casinos on American Indian reservations. Selected online links and resources help with research.

References and Bibliography

Abbott, J. (1996). A new synthesis for effective learning. *Wingspread Journal, 17*(2), 10–12.

Achilles, C. M., & Hoover, S. P. (1996, August). *Problem-based learning (PBL) as a school-improvement vehicle*. Paper presented at the annual meeting of the National Council of Professors of Educational Administration, Corpus Christi, TX. (ERIC Document Reproduction Service No. ED 401 631)

Albanese, M.A., & Mitchell, S. (1993). Problem-based learning: A review of literature on its outcomes and implementation issues. *Academic Medicine, 68*(1), 52–81.

Alkove, L., & McCarthy, B. (1992). Plain talk: Recognizing positivism and constructivism in practice. *Action in Teacher Education, 14*(2), 9–15.

Allen, D., Dion, L., & White, H. (2000, October). *Managing multiple groups: Peer facilitators as a solution*. Paper presented at the PBL 2000 Conference, Samford University, Birmingham, AL.

Alper, L., Fendel, D., Fraser, S., & Resek, D. (1996). Problem-based mathematics—not just for the college-bound. *Educational Leadership, 53*(8), 18–21.

American Association for the Advancement of Science, Project 2061. (1993). *Benchmarks for science literacy*. New York: Oxford University Press.

Aspy, D. N., Aspy, C. B., & Quinby, P. M. (1993). What doctors can teach teachers about problem-based learning. *Educational Leadership, 50*(7), 22–24.

Association for Supervision and Curriculum Development. (1997). *Problem-based learning series* [Two videotapes]. Alexandria, VA: Author.

Atkinson, B., Brown, J., & Ralls, M. B. (2000, October). *Designing a problem-based learning course: Educ 305 Teaching in the middle school*. Paper presented at the PBL 2000 Conference, Samford University, Birmingham, AL.

Barell, J. (1995a). Problem-based learning and crew members of the *Santa Maria*. In J. Barell (Ed.), *Teaching for thoughtfulness*. White Plains, NY: Longman.

Barell, J. (1995b). *Teaching for thoughtfulness: Classroom strategies to enhance intellectual development* (2nd ed.). New York: Longman Publishers. (ERIC Document Reproduction Service No. ED 381 514)

Barell, J. (1998). *PBL: An inquiry approach*. Arlington Heights, IL: IRI/SkyLight Training and Publishing.

Barrows, H., & Tamblyn, R. (1976). An evaluation of problem-based learning in small groups using a simulated patient. *Journal of Medical Education, 51*(1), 52–54.

Barrows, H. S. (1988). *The tutorial process*. Springfield, IL: Southern Illinois University School of Medicine.

Beane, J. (1993). *A middle school curriculum: From rhetoric to reality*. Westerville, OH: National Middle School Association.

Benoit, B. (1996). PBL and the summer youth jobs program. *The Problem Log, 1*(1), 4.

Bloom, B. S., & Krathwohl, D. R. (1956). *Taxonomy of educational objectives: The classification of educational goals by a committee of college and university examiners. (Handbook I: Cognitive Domain)*. New York: Longman & Green.

Bodner, G. (1986). Constructivism: A theory of knowledge. *Journal of Chemical Education, 63*(10), 873–877.

Boix-Mansilla, V., & Gardner, H. (1997). Of kinds of disciplines and kinds of understanding. *Phi Delta Kappan, 78*(5), 381–386.

Boud, D., & Feletti, G. (1991). *The challenge of problem-based learning*. New York: St. Martin's Press.

Brand, S. (Ed.). (1971). *The last whole earth catalog*. (Whole Earth Catalog Series). Menlo Park, CA: Portola Institute, Inc.

Bransford, J. D. (1993, April). *Who ya gonna call? Thoughts about teaching problem solving*. Paper presented at the annual meeting of the American Educational Research Association, Atlanta, GA.

Bredo, E. (1994). Cognitivism, situated cognition and Deweyan pragmatism. In M. S. Katz (Ed.), *Proceedings of the Fiftieth Annual Meeting of the Philosophy of Education Society.* Urbana-Champaign: University of Illinois, Philosophy of Education Society. Available (accessed July 15, 2001): http://w3.ed.uiuc.edu/EPS/PES-Yearbook/ 94_docs/BREDO.htm

Brooks, J. G., & Brooks, M. G. (1993). *In search of understanding: The case for constructivist classrooms* (1st ed.). Alexandria, VA: Association for Supervision and Curriculum Development.

Brooks, J. G., & Brooks, M. G. (1999). *In search of understanding: The case for constructivist classrooms* (2nd ed.). Alexandria, VA: Association for Supervision and Curriculum Development.

Brooks, M. G., & Brooks, J. G. (1999). The courage to be constructivist. *Educational Leadership, 57*(3), 18–24.

Broudy, H. (1982). What knowledge is of most worth? *Educational Leadership, 39*(8), 574–578.

Bybee, R. W. (1997). *Achieving scientific literacy: From purposes to practices.* Portsmouth, NH: Heinemann.

Casey, M., & Tucker, E. (1994). Problem-centered classrooms. *Phi Delta Kappan, 10*(94), 139–143.

Center for Problem-Based Learning. (1996a). *Professional development resource materials.* Aurora, IL: Illinois Mathematics and Science Academy.

Center for Problem-Based Learning. (1996b). Role playing in problem-based learning. [Online article]. Aurora, IL: Illinois Mathematics and Science Academy. Available (accessed July 15, 2001): http://www.imsa.edu/team/cpbl/instruct/Bisonproj/roleplng.html

Center for Problem-Based Learning. (1996c). "Why do mosquitoes buzz in people's ears?" Developed for the Harris Institute. Aurora, IL: Illinois Mathematics and Science Academy.

Center for Problem-Based Learning. (1997). *Problem-based learning: Three classrooms in action* [Videotape]. Aurora, IL: Illinois Mathematics and Science Academy.

Clark, C. M. (1988). Asking the right questions about teacher preparation: Contributions of research on teacher thinking. *Educational Researcher, 17*(2), 5–12.

Clarke, J. (1997). Solving problems. In J. Clarke & R. M. Agne (Eds.), *Interdisciplinary high school teaching.* Boston: Allyn and Bacon.

Cohen, E. G. (1994). *Designing groupwork: Strategies for the heterogeneous classroom* (2nd ed.). New York: Teachers College Press.

Cornbleth, C. (1988). Curriculum in and out of context. *Journal of Curriculum and Supervision, 3*(2), 85–96.

Covey, S. R. (1990). *The 7 habits of highly effective people.* Salt Lake City, UT: Franklin Covey Co.

Darling-Hammond, L., & Ball, D. L. (1997). *Teaching for high standards: What policymakers need to know and be able to do.* Philadelphia, PA: CPRE Publications/University of Pennsylvania.

Dean, C. D. (2000, October). *So how do we solve this problem? Making PBL work for your students.* Session presented at the PBL 2000 Conference, Samford University, Birmingham, AL.

Delisle, R. (1997). *How to use problem-based learning in the classroom.* Alexandria, VA: Association for Supervision and Curriculum Development.

Dewey, J. (1916). *Democracy and education: An introduction to the philosophy of education.* New York: Macmillan.

Dewey, J. (1943). *The school and society.* Chicago: University of Chicago Press.

Dewey, J. (1910/1991). *How we think.* Buffalo, NY: Prometheus Books. (Original work published 1910)

Dods, R. (1996). A problem-based learning design for teaching biochemistry. *Journal of Chemical Education, 73,* 225–228.

Doll, W. (1993). Curriculum possibilities in a "post"-future. *Journal of Curriculum and Supervision, 8*(4), 277–292.

Duffy, T. M., & Savery, J. R. (1995, February). *Constructivism: A theory of learning with implications for instruction.* Session presented at the annual meeting of the Association for Educational Communications and Technology, Anaheim, CA.

Eck, J. C., & Mathews, D. G. (2000). A sample of assessment findings related to Samford University's problem-based learning initiative. *PBL Insight, 3,* 3.

Erickson, D. K. (1999). A problem-based approach to mathematics instruction. *Mathematics Teacher, 92*(2), 516–521.

Farr, R. (1993). *How do you know a good one when you see one?* Presentation at the Annual Conference of the Illinois Association for Supervision and Curriculum Development. Bloomington-Normal, IL.

Finkle, S., Briggs, R., Hinton, L., Thompson, J., & Dods, R. (1994). *The summer challenge landfill problem.* Aurora, IL: Illinois Mathematics and Science Academy.

Fogarty, R. (1997). *Problem-based learning and other curriculum models for the multiple intelligences.* Arlington Heights, IL: IRI/SkyLight Training and Publishing.

Fosnot, C. T. (1989). *Enquiring teachers, enquiring learners: A constructivist approach for teaching.* New York: Teachers College Press.

Gallagher, S., Rosenthal, H., & Stepien, W. (1992). The effects of problem-based learning on problem solving. *Gifted Child Quarterly, 36*(4), 195–200.

Gibbons, D. (1995). *PBL diffusion: Factors influencing PBL knowledge, teaching values, and level of use.* Unpublished report available from the Illinois Mathematics and Science Academy, Aurora, IL.

Glickman, C. (1991). Pretending not to know what we know. *Educational Leadership, 48*(8), 4–10.

Glickman, C. (2000). The good and bad of standards. *Education Update, 42*(4), 1.

Greenberg, J. (1990). *Problem-solving situations* (Vol. 1). Corvallis, OR: Grapevine Publications.

Harris, K. R., & Graham, S. (1996). Memo to constructivists: Skills count, too. *Educational Leadership, 53*(5), 26–29.

Heathcote, D. (1983). Learning, knowing, and language in drama. *Language Arts, 60*(6), 695–701.

Heathcote, D., & Herbert, P. (1980). A drama of learning: Mantle of the expert. *Theory into Practice, 24*(3), 173–180.

Hendley, V. (1996, October). Let problems drive the learning. *AESS Prism,* 30–36.

Hewitt, J., & Scardamalia, M. (1996). *Design principles for the support of distributed processes.* Toronto: University of Toronto. Available (accessed July 15, 2001): http://twilight.oise.utoronto.ca/abstracts/distributed

Illinois Problem-Based Learning Network. (1996). *Don't let the smoke get in your eyes.* The Summer Sleuths Program. Aurora, IL: Illinois Mathematics and Science Academy.

Illinois State Board of Education. (1997, Summer). *Illinois learning standards.* Springfield, IL: Author. Available (accessed July 15, 2001): http://www.isbe.state.il.us/ils/standards.html

Illinois State Board of Education and Illinois Mathematics and Science Academy (IMSA). (1998). *Illinois Scientific Literacy Network: Scientific literacy grant coordination.* Aurora, IL: IMSA. Available (accessed July 15, 2001): http://www.imsa.edu/project/isln/

Illinois State Board of Education's Center for Scientific Literacy. (1994). *Scientific literacy program: Request for proposals.* Springfield, IL: Author.

Indiana State Board of Education. (2000, Summer). *Indiana's academic standards: 10th grade reading/language arts.* Indianapolis, IN: Author. Available (accessed July 15, 2001): http://ideanet.doe.state.in.us/standards/grade09-12_eng.html

International Society for Technology in Education (ISTE). (2000). *National educational technology standards for students—connecting curriculum and technology.* Eugene, OR: Author.

Kagan, S. (1994). *Cooperative learning.* San Clemente, CA: Kagan.

Kanstoroom, M., & Finn, C. E., Jr. (Eds). (1999). *Better teachers, better schools.* Washington, DC: The Thomas B. Fordham Foundation.

Keller, G. (2000, October). *Problem-based learning in a scientific methods course for non-majors.* Paper presented at the PBL 2000 Conference, Samford University, Birmingham, AL.

Kitchener, K. S. (1983). Cognition, metacognition, and epistemic cognition: A three-level model of cognitive processing. *Human Development, 26*(4), 222–232.

Kochanowski, P., Sage, S. M., & Shafii-Mousavi, M. (2000, October). *Project-based learning in mathematics in action: Learning perspectives.* Paper presented at the PBL 2000 Conference, Samford University, Birmingham, AL.

Kohn, A. (2000). *The case against standardized testing: Raising the scores, ruining the schools.* Portsmouth, NH: Heinemann.

Krathwohl, D. R., Bloom, B. S., & Masia, B. B. (1964). *Taxonomy of educational objectives: The classification of educational goals (Handbook II: Affective Domain).* New York: David McKay Co.

Krynock, K. B., & Robb, L. (1996). Is problem-based learning a problem for your curriculum? *Illinois School Research and Development Journal, 33*(1), 21–24.

Krynock, K. B., & Robb, L. (1999). Problem solved: How to coach cognition. *Educational Leadership, 57*(3), 29–32.

Lave, J., & Wenger, E. (1991). *Situated learning: Legitimate peripheral participation.* Cambridge, UK: Cambridge University Press.

Lederman, L. (1994). Give a small child a hammer and soon everything needs hammering. *Simulation and Gaming, 25*(2), 215–221.

Lipman, M. (1988). Critical thinking—What can it be? *Educational Leadership, 46*(1), 38–43.

Lipman, M. (1991). *Thinking in education*. New York: Cambridge University Press.

Mawhorr, S. (1996, December 20). Glendale Heights students, trustees discuss dance club. Glen Ellyn (IL) *Daily Herald*, p. 4.

McTighe, J. (1996, September). *Toward more thoughtful assessment: Principles and practices*. Session at Illinois Association for Supervision and Curriculum Development Research Conference, Naperville, IL.

Musial, D. (1996). Designing assessments in a problem-based learning context. *The Problem Log, 1*(2), 4–5.

Musial, D., & Hammerman, L. (1997). *Framing ways of knowing in problem-based learning*. Unpublished manuscript.

National Council for the Social Studies. (1997). *National standards for social studies teachers*. Waldorf, MD: Author.

National Council of Teachers of Mathematics (NCTM). (2000). *Principles and standards for school mathematics*. Reston, VA: Author.

National Research Council. (1996). *National science education standards*. Washington, DC: National Academy Press.

Newmann, F. (1990). Higher-order thinking in social studies: A rationale for the assessment of classroom thoughtfulness. *Journal of Curriculum Studies, 22*(1), 41–56.

Norris, S. P. (1985). Synthesis of research on critical thinking. *Educational Leadership, 42*(5), 40–45.

Orrill, C. H. (2000, April). *Designing a PBL experience for online delivery in a six-week course*. Paper presented at the annual meeting of the American Educational Research Association, New Orleans, LA.

Perkins, D. (1992). *Smart schools: From training memories to educating minds*. New York: The Free Press.

Perkins, D. (1993a). Teaching for understanding. *American Educator, 17*(3), 8.

Perkins, D. (1993b). *An apple for education: Teaching and learning for understanding*. Presentation at the Educational Press Association (EdPress) Conference, Philadelphia, PA.

Perkins, D. (1999). The many faces of constructivism. *Educational Leadership, 57*(3), 6–11.

Piaget, J. (1975/1985). *The equilibration of cognitive structures* (T. Brown & K. J. Thampy, Trans.). Chicago: University of Chicago Press. (Original work published 1975)

Pierce, J., & Jones, B. F. (1998). *Problem-based learning: Learning and teaching in the context of problems*. (Contextual Teaching and Learning Project). Washington, DC: U.S. Department of Education and the National School-to-Work Office. Available (accessed July 15, 2001): http://contextual.org/docs/5-PIER1.pdf

Pohl, L. (1996, December 30). Village may open dance club for teens. *Chicago Tribune*, p. 3.

Pohl, L. (1997, January 15). Class tackles tough issues with critical thinking. Glen Ellyn (IL) *Daily Herald*, sec. 5, p. 1.

Qin, Z., Johnson, D. W., & Johnson, R. T. (1995). Cooperative versus competitive efforts and problem solving. *Review of Educational Research, 65*(2), 129–143.

Reigeluth, C. M. (1994). The imperative for systemic change. In C. M. Reigeluth & R. J. Garfinkle (Eds.), *Systemic change in education*. Englewood Cliffs, NJ: Educational Technology Publications.

Resnick, L., & Nolan, K. (1995). Where in the world are world-class standards? *Educational Leadership, 52*(6), 6–11.

Riddings-Nowakowski, J. (November, 1981). *An interview with Ralph Tyler*. Occasional Paper #13. Kalamazoo: Western Michigan University.

Rorty, R. (1991). *Objectivity, relativism, and truth: Philosophical papers* (Vol. 1). Cambridge: Cambridge University Press.

Sage, S. M. (2000a). A natural fit: Problem-based learning and technology standards. *Learning and Leading with Technology, 28*(1), 6–12.

Sage, S. M. (2000b, April). *The learning and teaching experiences in an online problem-based learning course*. Paper presented at the annual meeting of the American Educational Research Association, New Orleans, LA.

Sage, S. M. (2001). Using problem-based learning to teach problem-based learning. In B. Levin (Ed.), *Energizing teacher education and professional development with problem-based learning*. Alexandria, VA: Association for Supervision and Curriculum Development.

Sage, S. M., Kochanowski, P., & Shafii-Mousavi, M. (2001). *Project-based learning in undergraduate mathematics: Learning perspectives*. Manuscript submitted for publication.

Sage, S. M., Krynock, K. L., & Robb, L. (2000). Is there anything but a problem? A case study of problem-based learning as middle school curriculum integration. *Research in Middle Level Education Annual, 23*, 149–179.

Sage, S. M., & Torp, L. P. (1997). What does it take to become a teacher of problem-based learning? *Journal of Staff Development, 18*(4), 32–36.

Savery, J. R., & Duffy, T. M. (1995). Problem-based learning: An instructional model and its constructivist framework. *Educational Technology, 35*(5), 31–35.

Scardamalia, M., & Bereiter, C. (1991). Higher levels of agency for children in knowledge-building: A challenge for design of new knowledge media. *The Journal of Learning Sciences, 1*(1), 38–68.

Schmoker, M., & Marzano, R. (1999). Realizing the promise of standards-based education. *Educational Leadership, 56*(6), 17–21.

Shafii-Mousavi, M., & Kochanowski, P. (1999, July). *Mathematics in action: Social and industrial problems.* Session presented at the Mathematics Throughout the Curriculum Conference, Bloomington, IN.

Simmons, R. (1994). The horse before the cart: Assessing for understanding. *Educational Leadership, 51*(5), 22–23.

Sobol, T. (1997). Beyond standards: The rest of the agenda. *Teachers College Record, 98*(4), 629–637.

Stepien, W., & Gallagher, S. (1993). Problem-based learning: As authentic as it gets. *Educational Leadership, 50*(7), 25–28.

Stepien, W. J., Senn, P., & Stepien, W. C. (2000). *The Internet and problem-based learning: Developing solutions through the Web.* Tucson, AZ: Zephyr Press.

Swink, D. (1993). Role playing your way to learning. *Training and Development, 47*(5), 91–97.

Sylwester, R. (1995). *A celebration of neurons: An educator's guide to the human brain.* Alexandria, VA: Association for Supervision and Curriculum Development.

Tanner, C. K., Galis, S. A., & Pajak, E. (1997). Problem-based learning in advanced preparation of educational leaders. *Educational Planning, 10*(3), 3–12.

Torp, L. T. (1996). *Planning a problem-based learning adventure.* Naperville, IL: Possibilities, Inc.

Torp, L. T. (2000). *Success Lab Learning Centers quality assurance program.* Chicago, IL: Success Lab, Inc.

Torp, L., & Sage, S. (1998). *Problems as possibilities: Problem-based learning for K–12 education* (1st ed.). Alexandria, VA: Association for Supervision and Curriculum Development.

Trevitt, A. C. F., & Pettigrove, M. (1995, February). *Toward autonomous criterion-referenced assessment and self-assessment: A case study.* Invited keynote paper at 2nd European Electronic Conference on Assessment and Evaluation: Recent and Future Developments. European Association for Research into Learning and Instruction, SIG Assessment & Evaluation (EARLI-AE) List. Administered via: listserv@nic.surfnet.nl.

Tyler, R. W. (1949). *Basic principles of curriculum and instruction.* Chicago: University of Chicago Press.

U.S. Department of Labor. (1991). *What work requires of schools: A SCANS report for America 2000.* Washington, DC: U.S. Government Printing Office.

Ulmer, M. B. (1999). Revolution or evolution in mathematics education? The USCS experience. *PBL Insight, 2*(3), 1, 4–5.

Vernon, D., & Blake, R. (1993). Does problem-based learning work? A meta-analysis of evaluative research. *Academic Medicine, 7,* 550–563.

Vitale-Ortlund, C. (1994). *Harris Institute for introduction to problem-based learning design products.* Aurora, IL: Illinois Mathematics and Science Academy.

von Glasersfeld, E. (1989). Cognition, construction of knowledge, and teaching. *Synthese, 80,* 121–140.

von Glasersfeld, E. (1993, April). *Radical constructivism: Teaching vs. training.* Paper presented at the annual meeting of the American Educational Research Association, Atlanta, GA.

Wagner, B. (1988). Research currents: Does classroom drama affect the arts of language? *Language Arts, 65*(1), 46–55.

Wiggins, G., & Jacobs, H. (1995, November). *Toward student understanding: Designing coherent curriculum, assessment, and instruction.* Restructuring Your School: Integrated/Thematic Curriculum and Performance Assessment Conference, National School Conference Institute, St. Louis, MO.

Wiggins, G., & McTighe, J. (1998). *Understanding by design.* Alexandria, VA: Association for Supervision and Curriculum Development.

Willems, J. (1981). Problem-based group teaching: A cognitive science approach to using knowledge. *Instructional Science, 10*(1), 5–21.

Witherell, C., & Noddings, N. (1991). *Stories lives tell: Narrative and dialogue in education.* New York: Teachers College Press.

Wolf, C., McIlvain, L., & Stockburger, M. (1992). Getting our students to think through simulations. *Contemporary Education, 63*(3), 219–220.

Index

Page numbers in italic refer to pages that contain figures.

ABOUT THE AUTHORS

Linda Torp is the chief education officer for Success Lab, Inc., of Chicago; former director for academic planning, research, and evaluation at the Illinois Mathematics and Science Academy in Aurora; and a facilitator for ASCD's Problem-Based Learning Network, PBL Net (Web site: http://www.imsa.edu/team/cpbl/pbln/). Torp has served as director for the Center for Problem-Based Learning and worked as a professional developer for many years in the areas of problem-based learning, integrated curriculum, and literacy. Her work in schools as an educator and consultant spans elementary through graduate levels. Torp can be reached at Success Lab, Inc., Suite 700, 1033 West Van Buren Avenue, Chicago, IL 60607; phone: 312-492-8730, ext. 237, toll-free: 1-800-KIDS LEARN; e-mail: ltorp@successlab.com (Success Lab's Web site: http://www.successlab.com).

Sara Sage is assistant professor of secondary education at Indiana University in South Bend. She has served as a special educator and teacher educator. Sage has conducted PBL research studies and has worked with numerous teachers at the Center for Problem-Based Learning and internationally. She has written several publications related to PBL in both K–12 and teacher education classrooms. Her interests in addition to PBL include professional development for teachers, human development and learning, and constructivist teaching and learning models. Sage can be reached at the School of Education, Indiana University-South Bend, P.O. Box 7111, South Bend, IN 46634-7111; phone: 219-237-6504; e-mail: ssage@iusb.edu.